Money and Spirit

What Others Are Saying

"Whether you are a math genius or someone who has never balanced a checkbook (like me), Heather Day's new book *Money and Spirit* reassures us that God wants to bring us joy, peace, and freedom from financial worry. Centering each chapter on a different fruit of the Spirit, Heather uses transparency, humor, and biblical insight to present a message of hope for all. Read *Money and Spirit*, and put your money where your heart is!"

Ken Blanchard, Bestselling Co-Author of *The New One Minute Manager* and *Simple Truths of Leadership*

"I love what Heather addresses in *Money and Spirit*! This is a much-needed discussion of the connection between our finances and our souls."

Brant Hansen, Radio host and Bestselling Author of *Unoffendable* and *The Men We Need*

"Money always yields fruit in our lives. The question is whether that fruit is rotten or redemptive. Heather Day has provided us with a guidebook for navigating our way through the lies and distortions of a world that yields only bad fruit, and toward an abundant life replete with fruit that will last. Using the fruit of the Spirit from Galatians, Heather unpacks Scripture and applies it to real-life, practical situations regarding our attitudes and decisions around money. Her themes of surrender, freedom, and joy provide a fresh perspective on this place in our lives where battles rage. The study guide is an added blessing for individuals and groups. If you have any questions, fears, or frustrations about the role money plays in your life as a follower of Jesus, read *Money and Spirit*."

R. Scott Rodin, Author of *The Steward Leader* and President of Rodin Consulting, Inc.

"I have had the honor of God moving me through the callings of lawyer, church planter, church pastor, denominational leader and now serve as a seminary president. In all those settings, a thread of finances and how people steward (or do not) linked these areas of life and discipleship. *Money and Spirit* pulls at that thread in wise and winsome ways. It can be used for personal devotions and small group discipleship while calling for a deeper dependence on the work of the Holy Spirit in our lives. I highly recommend *Money and Spirit* to you and for you to share it with others!"

Rev. Jul Medenblik, President, Calvin Theological Seminary

"In *Money and Spirit*, Heather Day presents a fresh, biblically based, and engaging invitation to link one's stewardship with the fruits of the Spirit. *Money and Spirit* is filled with practical insights and encouraging counsel noting that 'surrender' is not a sign of defeat, but a spiritual pathway to victory. So, grab a cup of coffee and a yellow marker, and enjoy this step-by-step journey to financial fulfillment!"

Dr. John C. Bowling, President Emeritus,
Olivet Nazarene University

"*Money and Spirit* is a special book that goes beyond just giving advice on how to handle money. Unlike other books that only talk about saving and investing, *Money and Spirit* shows us how to give our money worries to God and follow His path. *Money and Spirit* is perfect for anyone who wants to see a real change in how they think about and use money. If you want to feel more love, kindness, peace, and joy when it comes to your finances, *Money and Spirit* is the book for you."

Russell N. James III, J.D., Ph.D., CFP®, Author,
Researcher and Director of Graduate Studies in
Charitable Planning, Texas Tech University

"With the genius of a master storyteller, Heather Day draws our attention to the ancient truths of Scripture and the requirement of total surrender in our lives including how we think about, spend, and save money. If you want a better and exciting future, start with her book, *Money and Spirit*. The abundant life may be even better than you think!"

Phyllis Hendry Halverson, President Emeritus,
Lead Like Jesus

"*Money and Spirit* is a book centered on Holy Scripture and the Holy Spirit's inspirations for God-honoring stewardship. It can be used as a self-guided study, a conversation between married couples, or as part of a small-group gathering. The stories, reflections, prayers, and conversations remind us that everything we have and everything that we are belongs to God. This is a timely and important book for our families and churches. I heartily recommend it."

Rev. Zachary King, Ph.D., General Secretary, Christian
Reformed Church in North America

"*Money and Spirit* by Heather Day is a transformative guide that illuminates how surrendering our finances to the Holy Spirit can lead to profound spiritual and practical change. Day's insights invite us to move beyond worldly tactics and embrace a spiritual journey toward true financial freedom and peace. *Money and Spirit* is a must-read for both individuals and groups seeking to align their financial practices with their faith."

Rev. Scott Vander Ploeg, Senior Pastor of Sunlight Community Church and Founder and President of Multiply222 Network

"A life led by the Holy Spirit is not easy. It is hard to surrender all areas of life to Jesus Christ, certainly when it involves our finances—and even more so when you try to do the journey alone. Are you and your family or small group ready to reflect on the practical questions this study provides? Are you willing to be challenged to put everything finance-related in service of the Kingdom of God? If so, real change is possible; *Money and Spirit* will show you how."

Jos Snoep, President and CEO, Bible League International

"*Money and Spirit* is well-written, easy to read and full of Scripture with a great format that lends itself easily to discussion in a small group. It even has a suggested lesson plan for each of the seven chapters. While *Money and Spirit* is geared toward audiences of all ages, the last chapter, 'What's Your Story?' specifically references the impact of godly grandparents. They will find *Money and Spirit* quite useful in using their financial journey to influence the younger generation to follow biblical principles. It's a great book!"

Larry Fowler, Founder and CEO, Legacy Coalition

"Heather Day shines light on the spiritual factors at the root of financial problems. Most books focus on symptoms like debt, for example, so they don't really solve anything; they fail to address the heart issues that motivated the poor decisions the person made. And we have all made them. She does this with a great mix of stories, Scripture, stats, and a keen focus on surrender. That last piece, I have learned in my own journey, addresses the heart condition. I commend *Money and Spirit* to you to get your heart right."

Dr. Gary G. Hoag, President and CEO, Global Trust Partners

Money & Spirit

*Surrendering Our Finances
to the Work of the Holy Spirit*

HEATHER M. DAY

NASHVILLE

NEW YORK • LONDON • MELBOURNE • VANCOUVER

Money and Spirit

Surrendering Our Finances to the Work of the Holy Spirit

Published in New York, New York, by Morgan James Publishing. Morgan James is a trademark of Morgan James, LLC. www.MorganJamesPublishing.com

Proudly distributed by Publishers Group West®

Morgan James BOGO™

A **FREE** ebook edition is available for you or a friend with the purchase of this print book.

CLEARLY SIGN YOUR NAME ABOVE

Instructions to claim your free ebook edition:
1. Visit MorganJamesBOGO.com
2. Sign your name CLEARLY in the space above
3. Complete the form and submit a photo of this entire page
4. You or your friend can download the ebook to your preferred device

ISBN 9781636985152 paperback
ISBN 9781636985169 ebook
Library of Congress Control Number:
2024939973

Cover and Interior Design by:
Chris Treccani
www.3dogcreative.net

Author Photo by:
Slay the Day Photography

Morgan James PUBLISHING

Builds

with...

Habitat for Humanity® Peninsula and Greater Williamsburg

Morgan James is a proud partner of Habitat for Humanity Peninsula and Greater Williamsburg. Partners in building since 2006.

Get involved today! Visit: www.morgan-james-publishing.com/giving-back

To everyday heroes of faith who are living
the adventure of wholehearted surrender.

Contents

Foreword
by Haydn Shaw

Money and Spirit is the powerful exploration we all need regarding what God wants to do with us and our money.

Everyone needs to know the tactics of managing money—but this book isn't powerful because it teaches us to be good at our finances.

Everyone needs to manage debt—but this book isn't powerful because it helps us get out of debt (although it will probably help you do that).

Everyone needs to control their thinking about money—but this book isn't powerful because of positive self-talk techniques from the best cognitive therapy research.

As important as the topics might be, this book is powerful because of Heather's hope-filled message, taught from personal experience. Money troubles run much deeper than knowledge and tactics, but peace, joy and freedom are available for those who want it.

In *Money and Spirit*, Heather explains that our money troubles begin with misplaced affections. We prioritize and desire things that begin to dominate us. When our hearts are anxious, greedy, and self-focused, it's no wonder we feel and think about money in problematic ways.

Jesus put it simply: *"Where your treasure is, there your heart will be also."* Money isn't the issue; money spotlights where we've hidden our treasures.

Heather shares why the solution to our money frustrations, mistakes, pressures, worries, and crises is connected to the fruit of the Holy Spirit. If we are at peace, generous, and joyful, we will have a good relationship with our money. If we have faith in God and trust Him with everything, we will be content with our finances—whether we have a lot or a little.

With refreshing vulnerability, Heather takes us on a journey through the fruit of the Holy Spirit, helping us see what is going on in our hearts and minds. She shares her personal struggles with overspending and debt, and the stress that's put on her marriage. From her own experience and the stories of others, she shows how God's desire to grow His fruit in our lives makes meaningful change possible.

In my case, *Money and Spirit* helped me realize how often money has recently been in my thoughts. My wife Laurie and I have been good with money. We had stayed out of debt, built a retirement, and gave generously. We didn't think about money much until I left the high-paid corporate world of weekly travel for a less demanding stage of life. We were living on half as much without a regular paycheck, and I began thinking about money a lot. I even started waking up in the middle of the night with money on my mind.

Money and Spirit was a good reminder that I have been tempted to put my faith in a regular paycheck and effective budgeting more than God. No wonder I was thinking about it more!

It goes to show, no matter our age, how new or old our faith, or if we are financially set or barely hanging on, money can push out what the Holy Spirit is trying to do in our lives. Instead of love, joy, and peace, we get tension, discontent and anxiety.

Far too many people are consumed with thoughts about money, hampering their joy and intensifying their anxiety. This exploration of the fruit of the Spirit helped me, and I know it will help you.

Money and Spirit is a powerful book that will help you find freedom, no matter your stage in life or financial situation.

Haydn Shaw
Author of *Sticking Points: How to Get 5 Generations Working Together in the 12 Places They Come Apart* and *Generational IQ: Christianity Isn't Dying, Millennials Aren't the Problem, and the Future is Bright.*

Preface

> *"Remain in me, as I also remain in you. No branch can bear fruit by itself; it must remain in the vine. Neither can you bear fruit unless you remain in me."*
>
> **John 15:4**

When it comes to solving our financial problems, there's no shortage of advice! Spend less. Save more. Invest smart. Work harder.

The problem is: tactics are seldom enough. Without God's intervention, we quickly and repeatedly slip back into old, destructive patterns.

The way we view and manage our money often reflects an internal battle for control: our way versus God's way.

Left on our own, we really stink things up. Greed. Anxiety. Oppression. Waste. Instability. These are the nasty, bruised and rotten fruit produced by our selfish desires.

When we remain connected to the Vine, however, the sweetness of God's spiritual fruit is refreshing and unmistakable.

Love.

Joy.

Peace.

Patience.

Kindness.

Goodness.

Faithfulness.

Gentleness.

Self-control.

Money and Spirit is not a health-and-wealth promise or a guidebook full of strategies to reduce debt and achieve financial security.

Rather, this study is an invitation to put our money where our hearts are and surrender it all to Christ. It's an offer to give up the battle in order to experience God's joy, peace and freedom instead.

This is a journey of abiding in God's Holy Spirit, giving all of our burdens, fears and worries about money to Him.

Getting the Most Out of *Money and Spirit*

What you hold in your hands is difficult to quantify in format. Is it a daily devotional? Yes. Is it a personal journal? Yes. It is a group Bible study? Also, yes.

This book includes:

- An introduction from the author explaining her personal financial journey,
- Six chapters exploring each of the fruits of the spirit (as listed in Galatians 5), and
- a final chapter inviting you to consider how God might use your experience to inspire and encourage others.

Each chapter includes one or more of the following:

- **Pause and Reflect:** Questions to reflect on what you have read and how you do or don't see the fruit of the Spirit in your financial thoughts, behaviors and decisions. Journal lines are provided to jot down notes about what the Holy Spirit reveals to you.
- **Stories of Surrender:** Stories from real people who have experienced personal transformation as a result of surrendering their finances to Christ.
- **Prayer of Surrender:** This prayer is repeated throughout this book, and you'll notice that it

is nearly identical from chapter to chapter. (The only difference is the inclusion of the topic or fruit explored in that chapter.) The repetition of this prayer is intentional as we believe that surrender is a daily, discipline—not a one-time experience. May the words of this prayer settle in your heart, providing you with a simple way to talk to God about any financial struggle or decision you face, now and in the years to come.

- **Watch and Learn:** Many chapters have corresponding videos that reinforce the concepts covered throughout this book. These videos, which can all be found at MoneySpirit.org, provide a wonderful opportunity to further reflect upon what the Holy Spirit wants to teach you.

Discussion Guide

There is no need to walk this journey alone! Firmly believing that God created us for community, a Discussion Guide is also provided at the back of this book. You will find greater fulfillment, encouragement and accountability by linking up with others for this study.

For each chapter of the book, there is a corresponding discussion guide, which includes:

- Key Bible verses
- Discussion questions
- Prayer prompts
- Teaching videos about the fruit of the Spirit (chapters 1-6)

Turn to page 127 to find helpful tips for facilitating this study with your spouse, family, friends, church, or other small group.

Introduction
The Battle Within

> *For in my inner being, I delight in God's law, but I*
> *see another law at work in me, waging war against*
> *the law of my mind and making me a prisoner of*
> *the law of sin within me.*
>
> **Romans 7:22-23**

There we were, smack dab in the middle of the happiest place on earth, and neither of us were happy. I once heard that Disney World is the place where American families pay to go fight, and that was certainly the case with us.

It was a battle for the ages.

In one corner: me, a thirty-something educated woman with the fruits of love, peace and joy of God in her heart. Usually.

In the other corner: my three-and-a-half-year-old, strong-willed son who was doing everything within his 35 pounds of power to squeeze those spiritual fruits dry.

As I remember it, we spent a good 40 minutes or more tangling over control.

I'd pick him up and set him in a makeshift time-out chair. He'd let out a visceral scream of rebellion, stand up, walk away from the chair, then fold his arms in defiance. Time and again, I'd pick him up, set him *back* in the chair, and hope this time it would stick. Instead, he'd loudly reiterate his rage-filled revolt, repeating the cycle once more.

What initiated the conflict? I don't recall exactly. Probably the denial of an extra cookie or his preoccupation with an off-limits boundary.

This I *do* know for sure. At the heart of the struggle was the exact same issue of every conflict before and ever since: his will versus mine.

Here's the funny thing: *my* will in that moment was only for *his* good.

"When you're ready to quit this nonsense, we can chat," I told him. "Then we can both get on with our day."

But my son simply couldn't see past the moment. Instead, he chose to remain in bondage.

Determined to do things his own way, he missed out on all the fun that was just around the corner.

The Prophet of Applebee's

Truth is, my son was just a pint-sized example of the battle within us all.

It's one thing to miss out on an afternoon of kiddie rides and costumed characters. The stakes are much higher as adults—or at least they have been for me.

Far too often, I have found myself in the same struggle as the apostle Paul described in his letter to the Christians in Rome.

> *"Although I want to do good, evil is right there with me. For in my inner being, I delight in God's law, but I see another law at work in me, waging war against the law of my mind and making me a prisoner of the law of sin within me. What a wretched man I am! Who will rescue me from this body that is subject to death?"* *(Romans 7:21b-24)*

Same, Paul, same. What a wretched person *I* am! Who will rescue me?!

I remember one particularly wretched evening when the depths of my personal entrapment suddenly became clear. This time it was in the parking lot of a food-based amusement park: Applebee's Neighborhood Grill.

My husband and I had scheduled a rare date night alone, unaccompanied by our two young children. Nobody would be put in time out *that* evening—or at least that's what I thought.

As luck would have it, however, my husband, my best friend in the world, was in a particularly bad mood that evening. En route to "eatin' good in the neighborhood," he kept picking fights over the dumbest little things (in my mind).

Exasperated, I finally called him out on his attitude, just as he pulled into a parking space.

"What is *wrong* with you?!" I demanded. "I thought we were out to have a good time."

Well, that's all it took to open the floodgates. In an outburst of emotion, my husband confessed that the stress of our debt was eating him alive; he saw no hope of ever escaping financial ruin.

You see, when my husband and I got married, I inherited his name. He, on the other hand, inherited my credit card bills and student loans.

It was as my fiancé that he had first seen the warning signs of my credit card philosophy. Still in college, I'd told him I made only the minimum payments every month. He lovingly suggested that was a bad idea—that I should be paying it *all* off right away. I thought he was being unnecessarily uptight.

Then together as newlyweds, we bought cars, furniture and our very first home—which needed appliances, windows and a new air conditioner. Little by little, our minimum payments kept going up and up, and so did the stress. We were living paycheck to paycheck, and every time something broke down, we'd turn to our credit cards to bail us out.

By the night of our dinner outing, the burden of debt had reached its ominous peak.

Ironically, we were both making pretty good salaries for our ages, but most of our paychecks were going toward past mistakes. Thankfully, we weren't quite in crisis yet, but that night, I finally understood the gravity of it all. We were one minor catastrophe away from complete devastation.

It was a painful and necessary reality check. We were embarrassed and overwhelmed by the sum of it all. How had we made such a mess?

Not knowing what else to do, we prayed together, right there in the parking lot. It wasn't a long, memorable, or articulate prayer; I don't even remember exactly what we said. I think it went a little something like this…

"Oh, dear Jesus, we're a hot mess. We've done it all wrong. Our finances are a disaster, and we can't see our way out. Can you please, please, please help us?"

Moments after the "amen," we walked hand-in-hand to the Applebee's lobby. There, we ran into a friend I hadn't seen in years, sitting by his wife. When I asked him what they'd been up to, my friend said he and his wife had just come from a weeks-long financial literacy class at their local church.

"It's the smartest decision we ever made," he told us. "We used to fight about money all the time, but this has made such a difference! You guys should sign up for it. I highly recommend it."

My husband and I stared at each other in stunned silence, our jaws nearly hitting the floor. *Did that just happen?!*

To this day, that dinner date encounter remains the quickest and clearest answer to prayer that I've ever received.

What Have We Got to Hide?

Part of what made that conversation so astounding was that my friend dared to speak the taboo out loud.

You see, for reasons I can't quite comprehend, the word "money" is often treated as profanity within the church. We'll talk about how Jesus saves us from hatred, gossip, lies and betrayal. I mean, we'll even talk about

> **The word "money" is often treated as profanity within the church.**

overcoming booze, babes, binges, and bongs. But money? No way! That topic crosses the line.

Meanwhile, our collective financial troubles are creating bondage, division and devastation, both inside and outside the church walls.

Consider this:

- The average American holds a debt balance of $96,371 and spends roughly 9.58 percent of their disposable income on debt repayment, according to the latest data available.[1]

- One-third of U.S. born-again Christians say it is impossible for them to get ahead in life because of their personal debt.[2]
- Even winning the lottery doesn't ease burdens for the financially struggling. Approximately one-third of all lotto winners eventually declare bankruptcy.[3]
- What about other windfalls? The average person in their 20s-40s who receives a large inheritance almost immediately loses half of it through spending or poor investments.[3]
- According to the American Psychological Association, "compared to other touchy topics, couples' arguments about money tend to be more intense, more problematic and more likely to remain unresolved."[4]
- 59 percent of divorcees say that finances played at least "somewhat" of a role in their divorces (20 percent believe it played a "big" role). 36 percent say their spouse's credit score was a source of stress in their marriage.[5]

Church, we have a problem. So, why are we so afraid to talk about it?

Who Will Rescue Me?

In sharing about his financial journey, my friend unlocked a comforting realization that we were not alone—and that Jesus cared about our struggle. Not only that, but God had already paved the way to rescue us from our financial darkness.

So, what if we *all* broke the stigma, stopped hiding, and started asking for God's will to be done in the areas where we need Him the most?

Remember Paul's question about being rescued from his wretchedness? Clearly, it was rhetorical since he declared his firsthand experience in the very next verse.

"Thanks be to God, who delivers me through Jesus Christ our Lord!" (Romans 7:25)

Yeah, but does Jesus *really* care about our money? You better believe it! In fact, more of Jesus's recorded words refer to money than any other topic, including all His teachings on heaven and hell combined.

Here's just a sampling…

- *Then he said to them, "Watch out! Be on your guard against all kinds of greed; life does not consist in an abundance of possessions."* (Luke 12:15)

- *Then some soldiers asked him, "And what should we do? He replied, "Don't extort money and don't accuse people falsely—be content with your pay."* (Luke 3:14)
- *"Do not be afraid, little flock, for your Father has been pleased to give you the kingdom. Sell your possessions and give to the poor. Provide purses for yourselves that will not wear out, a treasure in heaven that will never fail, where no thief comes near and no moth destroys. For where your treasure is, there your heart will be also."* (Luke 12:32-34)

You see, money is not profanity in God's Kingdom, and it is certainly not beyond the scope of where He wants to be involved in your life.

Before you can get on the path toward healing, however, you must first wrestle with this most important question.

Are you ready to surrender to God's will for your money, or are you still determined to go your own way?

As long as you're fighting against God's good and perfect will, you can't ever experience the fulfilling life He's designed for you. Like my strong-willed toddler, you'll be choosing time-out bondage instead of the joy that's just around the corner.

As Jesus said, *"No one can serve two masters. Either he will hate the one and love the other, or he will be devoted to the one and despise the other. You cannot serve both God and money."* (Matthew 6:24)

Are you hurting, broken, scared and alone? Does the mere mention of money create tension in your chest or dissension in your relationships? Are you buried up to your eyeballs in debt or imprisoned by your past mistakes?

Boy, do I have good news for you!

There is hope for your situation. You are not alone. Jesus cares for you, and He's already provided the way out.

> *As for you, you were dead in your transgressions and sins, in which you used to live when you followed the ways of this world and of the ruler of the kingdom of the air, the spirit who is now at work in those who are disobedient. All of us also lived among them at one time, gratifying the cravings of our flesh and following its desires and thoughts. Like the rest, we were by nature deserving of wrath.*

> *But because of his great love for us, God, who is rich in mercy, made us alive with Christ even when we were dead in transgressions—it is by grace you have been saved. (Ephesians 2:1-5)*

The call to surrender it all to Christ is more than a get-out-of-hell-free card. Hope is more than Heaven.

God wants to bring you freedom—right here, right now—in the middle of whatever hopeless situation you face, including with your finances. You don't have to wait for a miraculous windfall, a get-rich scheme or a monetary hero to bail you out.

God wants to bring you freedom—right here, right now—in the middle of whatever hopeless situation you face.

Your true and loving Savior sees your mess, and He's already knocking at your door. So, will you answer His call?

Don't spend another day in bondage! There's freedom just around the corner.

Pause & Reflect

Take a moment to reflect on what you just read and what the Holy Spirit is revealing to you today.

- What is my visceral response when the topic of money comes up?
- How are finances affecting my emotional and mental health?
- In what ways are finances affecting my relationships with those around me? How about my relationship with the Heavenly Father?
- Am I ready for change?

_____

_____

_____

_____

_____

_____

_____

_____

_____

_____

_____

_____

_____

_____

_____

_____

_____

_____

_____

_____

_____

_____

_____

_____

Prayer of Surrender

Dear God,

I've made a mess of things! My ways have never been, and will never be, good enough. I need your rescue, please!

Thank you for paving the way to life through the death and resurrection of your Son.

I want to be in the center of your will, not mine, including with my finances. I surrender it all to you.

In Jesus's name, I pray,

Amen.

Notes

1. Gillespie, Lane. "Average American Debt Statistics." *Bankrate*, Jan. 13, 2023, www.bankrate.com/personal-finance/debt/average-american-debt/

2. Barna. "Why The Generations Approach Generosity Differently." June 19, 2019. www.barna.com/research/generations-generosity/

3. Sarwa. "How To Manage Sudden Wealth: 6 Steps To Protect and Grow Your Windfall." Accessed Feb. 20, 2024. www.sarwa.co/blog/how-to-manage-sudden-wealth

4. Experian. "How Much of a Role Do Finances Play in Divorce?" Feb. 14, 2017. www.experianplc.com/newsroom/press-releases/2017/how-much-of-a-role-do-finances-play-in-divorce

5. Klontz, Brad and Gresham, Mary. "Happy Couples: How to Avoid Money Arguments." American Psychological Association. Accessed Feb. 20, 2024. www.apa.org/topics/money/conflict

Chapter 1
Good Fruit Vs. Bad Fruit

> "But the fruit of the Spirit is love, joy, peace, forbearance, kindness, goodness, faithfulness, gentleness and self-control. Against such things there is no law."
>
> **Galatians 5:22-23**

It's become one of my most ridiculous, guilty pleasures. Watching *The Masked Singer* provides me with a level of joy and entertainment that I'm not sure I can quite explain.

In case you're not familiar with the show, here's the basic premise…

One by one, mystery celebrity contestants (and to be clear, we're using the term "celebrity" loosely here) walk out on the stage, introduced by a highly produced "clue package" video. Each contestant is cloaked in a stunning, over-the-top and often whacky costume. Some of my favorites have included an ice cream cone, a gangster toad and a giant singing head of broccoli.

Based on the clue package and their vocal performance, a panel of B-List celebrities is then tasked with selecting which "masked singer" will advance to the next round AND trying to determine each contestant's identity.

My favorite part, though, is anticipating what each contestant will sound like as they hit their first few notes. From their appearance, you can't possibly tell whether there's a Grammy award winner, Super Bowl champion, or social media influencer inside. Will their performance be heavenly, or will it be horrendous?

Call me crazy, but I prefer it when the visually stunning turns out to be a stinker.

Something Smells Rotten

Likewise, it's often difficult to tell the status of one's financial health from casual observation. From all outward appearances, we might seem put-together, happy, healthy and thriving, even as we're really stinking things up. Except, by the time we finally see the truth, it's no laughing matter at all.

In my case, it took nearly a decade of marriage before I was able to recognize the financial spoil. It was like biting into a beautiful, perfect-looking piece of fruit only to discover it was rotten at the core.

In his letter to the church in Galatia, Paul includes an infamous list of rotten fruit that's produced by our evil desires. Among them: immorality, discord, jealousy, fits of rage, selfish ambition, dissensions, factions, envy "and the like" (see Galatians 5:19-21).

It's not hard to identify the stench of this produce—we've all tasted their rot in our finances at one point or another. Yet, we can't seem to rid ourselves of money's bitterness, no matter how hard we try.

Maybe, like me, you've chosen to settle for lies and patterns that reek of sour decay:

- Debt.
- Greed.
- Secrets.
- Fears.
- Disappointments.
- Emptiness.

It's not a lot, but it's what we've got. There's just no changing it, right?

Money is Spiritual

What if I told you that you—yes you!—can have good fruit, not only in your finances, but deep down in your soul?

What if you found true peace and freedom?

What if you threw away your heartache, conflict, fears and regret in exchange for something sweeter?

All of this is possible when you choose to abide in the Spirit.

You see, for far too long, we have been conditioned to believe that money problems require only money solutions. Spend less. Save more. Invest smart. Work harder.

But that's a lie! Tactics are never enough.

Money is spiritual, and so our money problems require spiritual solutions.

Our financial lives reveal where we find our security, happiness and comfort.

Our financial lives reflect something much deeper. They reflect our spiritual condition. They expose who or what we love. They reveal where we find our security, happiness and comfort.

Yes, solid counsel and financial literacy are useful, but they'll only take us so far. Downloading a money app, taking a financial course, or creating an Excel spreadsheet can't possibly fix the issues of misplaced priorities and trust.

Unless we are changed at the heart level, we will always have distorted finances that reflect very little of God's original design for our wealth.

Our only true hope is found in the gift of the Holy Spirit, to whom we receive access at the very moment we surrender our lives to Jesus Christ.

> *"When you believed, you were marked in him with a seal, the promised Holy Spirit, who is a deposit guaranteeing our inheritance until the redemption of those who are God's possession—to the praise of his glory." (Ephesians 1:13b-14)*

Two thousand years ago, the apostle Paul challenged the believers in Galatia to make the life-altering decision of daily abiding in God's Spirit.

> *"So I say, walk by the Spirit, and you will not gratify the desires of the flesh. For*

> the flesh desires what is contrary to the Spirit, and the Spirit what is contrary to the flesh. They are in conflict with each other, so that you are not to do whatever you want. But if you are led by the Spirit, you are not under the law."
> (Galatians 5:16-18)

The power of his words, "walk by the Spirit," ring as true today as they did back then. They admonish us to choose wisely and to allow our hearts to be transformed. They encourage us to embrace the mind and heart of God about money, so we can live in the freedom He created for us.

The resulting sweetness of God's spiritual fruit is refreshing and unmistakable.

"But the fruit of the Spirit is love, joy, peace, forbearance, kindness, goodness, faithfulness, gentleness and self-control. Against such things there is no law."
(Galatians 5:22-23)

Let me ask you this…

How different would your financial life be if your daily money decisions were rooted in love, joy, peace, patience, kindness, goodness, faithfulness, gentleness and self-control?

Would you worry less about your finances?

Would you use your time differently?

Would you find more joy in giving and experience more peace over your future?

Let's Take a Journey!

Today, I invite you on a journey of daily surrender to Christ.

It's a journey of abiding in His Spirit, giving all your burdens, fears and worries about money to Him. It's allowing yourself to be transformed and to be part of the transformation of those around you, by putting your finances back into their proper place.

This journey doesn't promise financial abundance or overnight solutions to your problems. In fact, there are a few caveats you should know…

1. Surrendering to the work of the Holy Spirit isn't a get-rich scheme—or even a guarantee to get rich at all. Some of the most faithful, Spirit-led believers I've ever met barely had two nickels to rub together. Conversely, some of the world's most wealthy have no awareness of the Spirit's leading at all. There is

no direct correlation between one's spiritual health and their earthly net worth.

2. Health, wealth and happiness are fleeting—and yet God is faithful. If our faith is contingent on a smooth and painless journey, we'll miss out on the sweetness of God's presence through every circumstance. Just ask Job....

"...Naked I came from my mother's womb, and naked I will depart. The Lord gave and the Lord has taken away; may the name of the Lord be praised." (Job 1:21)

3. Following the Holy Spirit's guidance doesn't mean a quick and easy turnaround. Actually, in many cases, it's exactly the opposite as we commit to relearning patience, goodness and self-control.

But if you say "yes," you will experience peace that passes all understanding. You will find comfort in knowing that God loves you and wants what is best for you. He is your ultimate provider, and He can be trusted.

As you walk in obedience to God and surrender full control, your burdens will be lifted, regardless of your current situation or past mistakes. His spiritual fruit will grow in every area of your life, including in your finances.

You can replace greed and heartache with love and kindness. You can trade anxiety and strife for peace and joy.

> **The Holy Spirit offers real, lasting transformation— from the inside out.**

After all, the world's tactics and solutions will only get you so far. The Holy Spirit offers real, lasting transformation—from the inside out.

So, how about it?

You decide the kind of fruit you want to see in your finances. It can be bitter, or it can be sweet. What will you choose today?

Pause & Reflect

Take a moment to reflect on what you just read and what the Holy Spirit is revealing to you today.

- What is the current level of "freshness" in my finances? Are my thoughts and behaviors sweet, or are they stinky?
- Which spiritual fruit would I like to see more evidence of in my finances?

- Am I ready to surrender my finances to Christ, or am I determined to keep doing things my way?

_____

_____

_____

_____

_____

_____

_____

_____

_____

_____

_____

_____

_____

_____

_____

_____

_____

Prayer of Surrender

Spirit of God,

You are the source of life and blessing. It is only through you that I can bear good fruit that lasts. Therefore, I surrender myself to you today.

Specifically, I surrender my finances to you. Show me where there is rot and decay; rid me of anything that gets in the way of my connection to the Vine.

May your fruit be evidenced in my financial decisions today and throughout this week. Prompt me when my decisions are not in step with your perfect design. You can always be trusted, and so I will follow you today.

In Jesus's name I pray,

Amen.

"I Can't Take This Anymore"
Story of Surrender: Josh

"My mom did her best as a single mom, but we had nothing growing up," says Josh. "So, after high school, I went into the Marines thinking I would save her some money and get my college funded."

Two tours in Iraq later, Josh was broke in ways far beyond dollars and cents. "Coming home and dealing with the trauma of war, I felt completely separated from God," he recalls. "There was this void, and I tried to fill it in a lot of different ways."

Partying, alcohol, drugs and lots of reckless spending. It took five years of chasing illusions for Josh to finally reach the bottom.

"Driving on the interstate one day, I pulled my truck to the side of the road," says Josh. "I just said, 'God, I can't take this anymore. This is not me. I'm ready to surrender my life back to you.' And I never turned back after that."

One of the first tests of Josh's faith came when his new pastor talked to him about tithing.

"Frankly, I was offended," he says. "I thought, 'Here I am just trying to get back on track, and this guy's trying to get my money.' But then I remembered what I'd prayed on the side of that road. I realized this was a way to demonstrate I was serious about surrendering to God."

"I wrote out a check to my church for 10 percent of my income for that week," he continues. "Honestly, I worried if there was even enough in my account for the check to clear, but I just sensed God saying to me, 'Trust me.'"

The next day Josh came home to an unexpected check in the mail—reimbursement for a bill he had overpaid three months prior. "It brought this sense of relief; I knew God was going to take care of me."

Today, Josh and his wife, Laura, continue to trust and obey God in every aspect of their marriage. While climbing out of debt, paying off medical bills, and learning to live within their budget, they've listened closely to the Holy Spirit's leading.

It's a far cry from where Josh found himself as a young man.

"I was trying to portray an image, but I was hurting," says Josh. "I was mean, I was selfish, and I was lost. But today, I am full of joy. I love the Lord. I'm generous, and I'm happy."

Josh continues, "I surrendered my finances to the Lord, and he has brought more things into my life than I can ever say that I deserve. It's a total transformation."

Watch and Learn

Watch the video titled, "Good Fruit vs. Bad Fruit" found at MoneySpirit.org for further teaching and reflection.

Chapter 2
Love

> *Whoever loves money never has enough; whoever loves wealth is never satisfied with their income. This too is meaningless.*
>
> **Ecclesiastes 5:10**

The small-but-mighty book of Haggai begins like a therapist's intervention. Looking into his clients' … errrr, I mean the Hebrews'… eyes, Haggai's questions unveiled the true issue at play.

"And how does that make you feel?" he questioned—albeit in ancient terminology.

Unphased by the awkward silence, Haggai let them squirm on the biblical couch for more than just a few moments. Then, on behalf of God, he recounted their behavioral evidence, allowing them to draw their *own* conclusions about the state of their mental health.

> *"Now this is what the Lord Almighty says: 'Give careful thought to your ways. You have planted much, but harvested little. You eat, but never have enough. You drink, but never have your fill. You put on clothes, but are not warm. You earn wages, only to put them in a purse with holes in it.'" (Haggai 1:5-6)*

In other words, "Let's get real," said Haggai. "Your stuff is NOT making you happy. It never has; it never will."

Haggai's prophetic assessment uncovered a searing void in Israelite living. It didn't matter what or how much they had; everyday life just wasn't right. There should have been fullness and gladness. Instead, they were empty inside.

They sought love, hope and security in their possessions. Instead, they should have focused their attention on the Giver of it all.

What's Your Stuff Telling You?

Much like the Israelites, we could all learn a thing or two about our emotional psyche by considering what our possessions tell us…

Each time your stuff doesn't solve your problems, pay attention.

After you're left bored by collections that used to thrill you, listen.

When you're hurt by people who don't like you because of the money you do or do not have, take note.

Our money is meant to be used, enjoyed and shared for God—not become our life's pursuit.

Our possessions remind us that our hearts belong to more than just trinkets and treasures. We are made for a deep and lasting relationship that begins with our worship of God.

At the end of the day, our money is meant to be used, enjoyed and shared for Him—not become our life's pursuit.

You see, for many of us, our approach to money reveals a deeper longing: to be seen, to be known, to feel safe, and ultimately, to be loved. Whether or not we recognize it, our financial decisions may reflect a piece of our hearts that's never been quite filled.

Distorted Views on Love

The effects of feeling unloved at any age—but especially in childhood—are profound, pervasive and long-lasting. Countless studies have shown a direct correlation between brain development in the early years and our social, emotional and behavioral traits as adults. This undoubtedly affects how we view and manage our money.

In a report for the *Wall Street Journal*, journalist Kate Murphy details how poor fiscal behaviors often reflect unhealed relationships and distorted views about love. She writes:

> *"Psychological, behavioral and neuroscience research indicates that how stable and secure you feel in your interpersonal relationships tends to mirror how stable and secure you feel about your finances. So, it's worth examining your close ties, both past and present, to understand how they may influence your spending, saving and investing*

habits—for good, or for ill.

"This doesn't necessarily involve hours on a psychoanalyst's couch, but it does require some honest self-reflection about your relationship history (starting with mom and dad) and the role money inevitably played. Money is tangled up with love in your subconscious. Indeed, getting and losing money activates the same pleasure and pain centers in the brain, respectively, as falling in love and having your heart broken.

"Depending on your background, you may come to associate intimacy— and money by proxy—with safety, peril, protection, secrecy, control, prestige, power, weakness, virtue, vice, acceptance or rejection. These often-dysfunctional associations are typically established early in life and are hard to shake, likely because you don't even know you have them."[1]

The long-term effects of a void in affection are widely documented and unmistakable. Children who felt unloved eventually become adults who exhibit one or more universal traits:

1. Insecure attachment style.
2. Undeveloped emotional intelligence.
3. Lack of trust.
4. Difficulties navigating boundaries.
5. Choosing toxic friends and partners.
6. Dominated by fear of failure.
7. Feelings of isolation.
8. Extreme sensitivity.

Clinical or not, stable households or not, most of us can at least partially relate to some of these emotional dysfunctions, including in our financial behaviors.

Maybe your childhood was amazing. Maybe it felt like hell on earth. Maybe you're like most of us for whom it was somewhere in between.

Regardless of our upbringing, most of us have felt the sting of abandonment, isolation or unworthiness at one time or another. This craving for love can creep into our financial lives in several unhealthy ways.

Have you ever…

- Attempted to buy the affection of others through extravagant gifts?
- Measured your self-worth on how much money is in your bank accounts?
- Overspent on clothes, collectibles or hobbies in search of a feels-like-love dopamine hit?
- Hoped your fancy home, car or toys would impress your friends, family or neighbors?
- Hoarded or saved excessively so you'll never have to go without or depend on others?
- Turned down the help of friends or family because you didn't want to appear needy?
- Gave or loaned to friends and family beyond what you had the reasonable capacity to give?
- Allowed others to dictate your spending decisions or take advantage of healthy financial boundaries?
- Dressed your kids in the latest fashions to protect their (or perhaps your) reputation?
- Gave in ways that led to resentment or came with strings attached?

It doesn't matter how exactly this bad fruit appears in our lives. If you answered "yes" to any of these questions, your heart is probably longing for something more.

Here's the hard truth: finances will never fill the void for affection. When you put your trust in money, all you'll be is broke.

Broken heart.

Broken dreams.

Broken relationships all around.

Finding True Love

There is hope and healing for the unloved, but it starts with recognizing and acknowledging the problem.

Ask our buddy Haggai or any of his modern-day counterparts: You can't be helped until you ask for help. To find and experience true love, you first must slam the door on your toxic relationship with money.

> When you put your trust in money, all you'll be is broke.

So how do you find your heart's truest desire? (Hint: It's not downloading a financial version of a dating app.)

1. Examine your heart.

Carve out time and space to consider what your money decisions reveal about who or what you love, how you determine your worth, and where you find your security.

One helpful place to begin is by conducting a financial inventory:

- How many credit card statements are piling up on your counter, and what's on the latest statements?
- What were your last 20 or so transactions from your checking account?
- How many Amazon boxes are piled up in your garage, and what's in your online cart right now?
- What are you hoarding or saving in excess of what you actually need to live comfortably?

Yes, our monetary decisions reflect our innermost desires. Or as Jesus so eloquently put it: *"For where your treasure is, there your heart will be also."* (Matthew 6:21)

In your exploration of your relationship with money, don't be afraid to ask for the support of a friend, mentor, pastor or therapist. Matters of the heart are often complicated and deeply rooted. More often than not, it helps to have an experienced and qualified guide to help you identify the path toward healing.

2. Abide in God's unconditional love.

God loves you—truly, madly, deeply. Do you really understand that? Do you believe that deep down in your soul?

There is absolutely nothing you can do to make God love you more. There is nothing you can do that will make Him love you less. His love is unbound, unconditional and unchanging.

> You are enough, and He is more than enough for you.

Regardless of what healthy relationships you have or have not had, regardless of your financial status or past mistakes, He loves you. I mean, He REALLY loves you—exactly as you are.

You are enough, and He is more than enough for you.

Even as I type this, I echo the apostle Paul's prayer for the Ephesians, that you, dear reader, would fully understand, receive and abide in His love.

> *"I pray that out of his glorious riches he may strengthen you with power through his Spirit in your inner being, so that Christ may dwell in your hearts through faith. And I pray that you, being root-*

ed and established in love, may have
power, together with all the Lord's holy
people, to grasp how wide and long and
high and deep is the love of Christ, and to
know this love that surpasses knowledge
— that you may be filled to the measure
of all the fullness of God."
(Ephesians 3:16-19)

As the love of God flows down and through every part of your life, you'll experience a confidence and security you've never known. His perfect love will cast out all fear. His love will compel and sustain you.

You won't need to look for your self-worth in what you own, how much money you make, or the image you've been desperately trying to keep. You certainly won't need to go into debt to try and gain acceptance.

Why is that? Because you'll know—really know, deep down—that God loves you. No. Matter. What.

Because the God of all Creation treasures you, you'll find your worth in Him.

3. Share His love with others.

God's love is unconditional—but it does not leave us alone.

When we truly experience the life-altering love of God, the Holy Spirit begins to mold and shape us, from the inside out. The Holy Spirit changes the way we think and how we see the world. Our priorities, decisions and behaviors are altered, making us more like Christ.

God's love compels us to move beyond the walls of our homes and outside our comfort zones. His love was never meant to be kept to ourselves.

God wants us to be agents of restoration, drawing others back into meaningful relationships with Him. Every day, every dollar He gives us is designed to be used for His glory and for reconciliation with His beloved creation.

As we begin to reflect on the heart and mind of Christ, we'll be drawn to share that endless love with everyone we know.

Instead of selfishness, we'll grow in *selfless* concern for others.

Instead of using money as a means of control, we'll see it as a tool to bless and encourage the people in our lives.

Instead of hoarding and saving for the great unknown, we'll ask how our God-given resources can be used for His glory and for the greater good.

When you abide in the Spirit, His love changes *everything*.

You won't have to wonder if the fruit of your financial endeavors is good. You'll be able to taste it for yourself.

Pause & Reflect

Take a moment to reflect on what you just read and what the Holy Spirit is revealing to you today.

- In what ways have I tried to use stuff to fill a void in my heart?
- Do I truly believe deep down within my soul that Jesus loves me, no matter what?
- How might God want to use my money to bless and show His love to others?

_____

_____

_____

_____

_____

_____

_____

_____

_____

_____

_____

_____

_____

_____

_____

_____

_____

A Love Letter from God

There are many, many verses throughout the Bible that say or illustrate just how much God cares for you. Read this letter—a small compilation of those verses—once, twice or as many times as it takes for you to truly soak it in. As you do, insert your name, allowing His words to speak directly to your heart.[2]

Dear _____,

I knit you together in your mother's womb. You are fearfully and wonderfully made.[a]

_____, I have loved you with an everlasting love; I have drawn you with unfailing kindness.[b] I loved you so much that I gave my one and only Son so that you shall not perish but have eternal life.[c]

I will never leave you, nor forsake you, _____.[d] Neither death nor life, neither angels nor demons, neither the present nor the future, nor any powers, neither height nor depth, nor anything else in all creation, will be able to separate you from my love that is available through Christ Jesus.[e]

So, cast all your cares on me, _____, because I care for you.[f]

And this is my commandment: Love one another. As I have loved you, so you must love one another.[g] Not with words or speech, but with actions and in truth.[h]

Love is patient, love is kind. It does not envy, it does not boast, it is not proud. It does not dishonor others, it is not self-seeking, it is not easily angered, it keeps no record of wrongs.[i]

And all this is possible because of my love that has been poured into your heart, through the Holy Spirit.[j]

With all my love,

God

Prayer of Surrender

Spirit of God,

You are the source of life and blessing. It is only through you that I can bear good fruit that lasts. Therefore, I surrender myself to you today.

Specifically, I surrender my finances to you. May I grow in understanding of the depths of your love, and may Your love be evidenced in my financial decisions today and throughout this week.

Prompt me when my decisions are not in step with your perfect design. You can always be trusted, so I will follow you today.

In Jesus's name I pray,

Amen.

"We Were Not Alone"
Story of Surrender: Lance and Amy

California dreamin'. This was the lifetime plan for newlyweds Lance and Amy, two pastors' kids who were born and raised on the Pacific coast.

"Our families are there; the weather was gorgeous; we had good jobs," says Amy. "We just knew this was going to be our forever home."

Until it all began to unravel.

The housing market crash left them with an upside-down mortgage, and ultimately, foreclosure. Then, they discovered Amy's banking information had been compromised, making her the victim of thousands of dollars in identity theft.

"It was stressful; it was hard, but there was peace in knowing God is faithful," says Amy. "He loves us. He cares for us. We knew that we were not alone, and that we were going to be okay."

Lance and Amy recall the variety of loving ways God provided for them. Unexpected refunds. Random insurance checks. Surprise bonuses. They began a three-year journey of relying on God's provision and surrendering their future to wherever God would lead them.

"We began to feel this tension that's really hard to explain," says Lance.

"We just really felt like God was changing our path," adds Amy, "like He was trying to prepare us for something bigger."

One day, Lance came home with a startling revelation. At the time, he had three jobs—teaching, coaching and working part-time as a youth pastor for their church.

"I had a very clear sense that God was asking me to resign from it all," says Lance. "We had a one-year-old and a baby on the way—so you can imagine how that conversation went."

"It was a step-out-of-the-boat faith moment for both of us," adds Amy. "Everyone thought we were crazy, but we both knew this was what God wanted us to do—even if we didn't know why."

Their answer came in the form of an out-of-the-blue phone call from a Christian university in Illinois. The dean on the other end of the line asked if Lance would consider joining the faculty.

"It was a perfect fit," says Amy.

Taking a leap of faith, they loaded up all their belongings and headed toward the Midwest. Soon after settling, Amy was hired as a children's pastor just 10 minutes away from the university.

Looking back, Lance and Amy see countless examples of God's love at work.

"It's amazing how God orchestrated all the details," says Lance. "Things that happened a decade ago are still working out in our lives, and in the lives of our children and our church."

"I'm so glad we followed God's plan and not our own," agrees Amy. "He uses all things, even bad situations, for good. God was moving us to the place where we were meant to be, serving Him in a different way."

"Sometimes people see God as someone who is above and far away and not actively present in our lives," she continues, "but that's not the case at all. He literally sent His own Son to walk among us because He loves us. He wants to be relational."

And together, Lance and Amy strive to show that love in their home, church and community. Whether it's their time, talents or treasure, they share what they have—freely and often—whenever the Lord prompts them to give.

"We have experienced God's love over and over again," concludes Amy. "It's only natural to take that and love other people well."

Watch and Learn

Watch the video titled, "Love" found at MoneySpirit.org for further teaching and reflection.

Notes:

1. Murphy, Kate. "Love and Money — And How They're Connected." *The Wall Street Journal*. Nov. 21, 2020. www.wsj.com/articles/love-and-moneyand-how-theyre-connected-11605917843

2. See: a. Psalm 139:13-14; b. Jeremiah 31:3, c. John 3:16; d. Hebrews 13:5; e. Romans 8:38-39, f. 1 Peter 5:7; g. John 13:34; h. 1 John 3:18; i. 1 Corinthians 13:4-5; j. Romans 5:5

Chapter 3
Joy and Peace

> "Come to me, all you who are weary and burdened, and I will give you rest. Take my yoke upon you and learn from me, for I am gentle and humble in heart, and you will find rest for your souls. For my yoke is easy and my burden is light."
>
> **Matthew 11:28-30**

When my kids were little, I frequently read to them from a children's book of brightly illustrated Bible stories. One of their favorite stories was that of Paul and Silas in jail. (See Acts 16:16-40.)

Imprisoned for proclaiming the Gospel, Paul and Silas decided to pass the time by doing what they did best: praising God. As they sang hymns, the prison walls began to shake and soon came crumbling down. The power of God had freed them.

One night after reading this story, my son (who was five at the time) declared, "I wish *I* could praise God like that!"

Before you assume him a preschool saint, I knew what he *really* wanted was the magical power to shake down walls at his command. (One of his favorite activities at that age was "using the force" every time we walked through automatic sliding doors.)

Still, his childish declaration is ultimately my heart's desire, too.

I want to praise God like Paul and Silas when the walls are high, the chains are tight, the bills are piling up, and the car is falling apart. I want to have unrelenting joy and unshakeable peace, regardless of what circumstances I happen to face today.

Except on some days, that's so much harder to do than others.

Financial Health Crisis

There is arguably no greater circumstance that steals our joy and peace than when we're in financial bondage.

A recent CreditWise survey revealed that finances were the number one source of stress for Americans (reported by 73% of respondents), beating out politics (59%), work (49%) and family (46%).[1]

The physical and emotional toll of this financial stress is obvious and can manifest itself in several destructive ways:

- Broken relationships
- Social withdrawal
- Depression
- Anxiety
- Panic attacks
- Unhealthy coping methods, such as heavy drinking, overeating, drug abuse or gambling
- Insomnia
- Excessive weight gain or loss
- A host of other physical maladies, including headaches/migraines, muscle tension, high blood pressure, diabetes, gastrointestinal problems, compromised immune systems and heart disease

According to Forbes, individuals with high financial stress are twice as likely to report poor overall health and four times more likely to complain of physical ailments.[2] What's more, all these conditions are often intensified when sufferers delay or avoid healthcare to minimize mounting medical bills.

Left unchecked, financial anxiety can even lead to mental health crises, including self-harm or suicidal thoughts. A 2021 survey by Student Loan Planner found that one in 14 student loan borrowers had considered suicide at some point during their repayment journey.[3]

To sum it all up: everything hurts, and we're dying.

A Roadmap from Paul

In a world where financial troubles are growing faster than the speed of inflation, how can we *possibly* find true peace and joy?

Singin' in the Jail artist Paul the apostle says it's not only *possible* but imperative.

In his letter to the Philippians, Paul writes, "*Rejoice in the Lord **always**. I will say it again: Rejoice!*" (Philippians 4:4, emphasis added)

To be clear, Paul's instruction is not to adopt a Pollyanna "just-smile-and-nod-and-everything-will-be-fine" mindset.

Instead, he lays out a roadmap to finding true joy and contentment in every circumstance.

1. Present your requests to God.

Paul writes, *"…The Lord is near. Do not be anxious about anything, but in every situation, by prayer and petition, with thanksgiving, present your requests to God."* (Philippians 4:5-6)

Are your financial troubles consuming your thoughts?

Are you in a dark hole of debt and you can't see a way out?

Are you afraid that if anyone *really* knew what was going on, they'd never look at you the same?

You are not alone. You don't have to do this by yourself.

Tell God about it.

All of it.

God sees all, and He knows all. What have you got to hide?

There is freedom in voicing your biggest worries and your deepest shame to the Father who loves you and is there to guide you through this journey.

You are not alone. You don't have to do this by yourself.

Jesus himself offers an invitation to all those who are stumbling under the weight of heavy bondage.

"Come to me, all you who are weary and burdened, and I will give you rest. Take my yoke upon you and learn from me, for I am gentle and humble in heart, and you will find rest for your souls. For my yoke is easy and my burden is light." (Matthew 11:28-30).

2. Build habits of gratitude.

Read those instructions from Paul again:

*"…in every situation, by prayer and petition, **with thanksgiving**, present your requests to God."*
(Philippians 4: 6b, emphasis added.)

Did you catch that? Present your requests with thanksgiving!

Modern psychology continues to reaffirm what Scripture has always instructed. Viewing our circumstances through a lens of gratitude rewires our brain, brightens our outlook, and changes our behaviors.

That's why it's a fundamental therapeutic process to repeatedly ask patients with anxiety, depression and addictions to identify reasons to be thankful. Addiction recovery programs almost always include the assignment of "daily gratitude lists," which help patients build new, healthy cognitive habits.

Ask the Holy Spirit to guide you in finding small, simple ways to practice gratitude, consistently and repeatedly. Much like walking, riding a bike or shooting a free-throw, gratitude is a positive habit that will become more and more natural with practice.

For example...

- Write a daily list of things for which you're grateful, whether that's family, friends, your home, health, the sunshine, or even that you managed to go a full day without stubbing your toe.
- Exercise your senses, using them as a cue to practice gratitude. What do I see that I'm grateful for? What do I hear? Smell? Taste? Touch?
- Celebrate financial victories, big and small. For example, "We finally paid off our Amazon bill!" or "I've finally saved up enough for those new shoes!" or "I managed to walk through Marshall's and *not* buy any of the trinkets in the checkout aisle!"

The more you allow the Holy Spirit to open your eyes to the good around you, the more natural and transformative the habit will become.

3. Redirect your thinking.

Consider this: What is your big *why* for surrendering your finances to Christ?

Are you only interested in managing and reducing the pain? Or do you long for something more?

Like a recovering addict who can't stop thinking about the drink they can't have, we often become so hyper-focused on our money problems that we completely miss seeing what's possible.

Paul implores us to lift our eyes away from our earthly struggles and focus instead on spiritual opportunities.

"Finally, brothers and sisters, whatever is true, whatever is noble, whatever is right, whatever is pure, whatever is lovely, whatever is admirable—if anything is excellent or praiseworthy—think about such things." (Philippians 4:8)

Ask yourself…

- How does God want to work in and through you on this financial journey?
- What does He want to teach you?
- How does He want to refine you?
- What would it do for your relationship with God, if you relied solely on Him for peace and joy?

- How many noble, right, pure and lovely ways might He use your money if you fully entrusted the management of it to Him?

Think about these things! Don't become so well-accustomed to looking into the darkness that you forget to turn toward the light.

> Don't become so well-accustomed to looking into the darkness that you forget to turn toward the light.

There's so much more that God wants to do for you than just pulling you out of the pit!

4. Get help.

We know, of course, that as Christ's followers we have the constant abiding presence of the Holy Spirit. Additionally, God, in all His love and wisdom, designed us for community.

Introvert or extrovert, it doesn't really matter. God created *YOU* to be at your best in relationships. In healthy relationships, we are affirmed, refined, bolstered, corrected, supported, equipped and loved.

Paul modeled this kind of relational support with the Philippians.

"Whatever you have learned or received or heard from me, or seen in me—put it into practice." (Philippians 4:9a)

If you're trying to walk this financial journey on your own, you're going about it all wrong!

First and foremost, enlist the love and support of those you care about the most.

If you are married, getting on the same page with your spouse is essential to your long-term financial health. If you remain at odds with one another, you're sunk before you even set sail.

If you're not married, it might mean turning to the trusted support of a parent, sibling, adult child, or a long-time friend. Think about those people who have consistently loved you no matter what. Trust that they will continue to do so, even at your financial worst.

It starts with getting real with one another. Really real. Like, I'm-going-to-tell-you-about-my-daily-coffee-splurges, my secret credit card, or my biggest financial fears, kind of real.

That kind of vulnerability is, in a word, terrifying! I remember how scary it was to confess my overspending to my husband that night in the Applebee's parking lot. I remember how emotional he was, more than I'd ever seen him before, as he verbally vomited his deepest fears.

But here's the pay-off, that I can tell you about first-hand…

There is a unique brand of relational intimacy that only comes with trust and vulnerability. No more secrets. No more lies. We're in this together—no matter what. That kind of transparent unity is extraordinarily powerful!

Second, seek out the help of a financial expert, someone who is trained and equipped to help you succeed in the practical matters of budgeting, paying off debt, saving and investing.

A person with that kind of expertise can help jumpstart your financial turnaround in several ways, such as:

- Teaching you money management skills
- Helping you identify the types of accounts and tools that will help you accomplish your goals
- Exploring options for efficient debt repayment
- Showing you how to apply for assistance, as needed.

Here's the good news: Financial expertise has never been more readily available. It might take the form of one-on-one consultations with a financial advisor. Alternatively, you might tap into the wide variety of books, podcasts, in-person workshops and/or online courses that are out there.

It's hard to go wrong when looking for basic financial training, since most are guided by universal principles around budgeting, saving and investing. However, it's most beneficial to look for people and resources guided by Christian values. After all, the end goal for believers is not about financial security and domination. Instead, the Spirit-led Christian is driven by how they can best steward their God-given resources for His glory.

Finally, in your financial journey, you may need the kind of emotional, relational or psychological support that only a trained mental health professional can provide.

Many of our money decisions are driven by deeply rooted longings or fears. You may be experiencing anxiety, depression, anger or other emotional pain due to hurt or trauma from the past. Perhaps your financial struggles are merely the symptom of a hurt that needs more healing.

Likewise, many couples—regardless of their level of faith or commitment to one another—find it nearly impossible to see eye-to-eye on money matters. Money is the number one cause of arguments between spouses, and it is among the top reasons cited by couples who ultimately file for divorce.

If you can't seem to talk about finances without it turning into a fight, you're in good company—but it doesn't have to stay this way.

A professional marriage counselor or mediator can help you identify new ways of communicating with one

The call to surrender is not a one-time thing.

another, gain mutual respect and understanding, and emerge standing on common ground.

5. Surrender again.

The call to surrender is not a one-time thing, but a daily—perhaps hourly—spiritual discipline. Every time we are tempted, angry, remorseful or afraid, we are picking back up what we've already laid down at the feet of God.

Paul reminds us that *"...the God of peace will be with you."* (Philippians 4:9b)

God carries us throughout this winding journey, and He patiently invites us to surrender our burdens to Him, again…and again…and again…and again. Peace and joy are not final destinations, but the fruit of abiding close to the Vine.

Bringers of Peace and Joy

But back to Paul and Silas…

Cracked shackles and opened prison doors were not the only miracles they experienced because of their heavenly jailhouse rock. The prison guard was so astounded by their peace and joy under the circumstances that he wanted to experience it for himself.

> "About midnight Paul and Silas were praying and singing hymns to God, and the other prisoners were listening to them. Suddenly there was such a violent earthquake that the foundations of the prison were shaken. At once all the prison doors flew open, and everyone's chains came loose. The jailer woke up, and when he saw the prison doors open, he drew his sword and was about to kill himself because he thought the prisoners had escaped. But Paul shouted, 'Don't harm yourself! We are all here!'
>
> "The jailer called for lights, rushed in and fell trembling before Paul and Silas. He then brought them out and

asked, 'Sirs, what must I do to be saved?'

"They replied, 'Believe in the Lord Jesus, and you will be saved—you and your household.' Then they spoke the word of the Lord to him and to all the others in his house. At that hour of the night the jailer took them and washed their wounds; then immediately he and all his household were baptized. The jailer brought them into his house and set a meal before them; he was filled with joy because he had come to believe in God—he and his whole household." (Acts 16:25-34)

You see, when we have peace and joy in spite of our circumstances, people tend to notice! It's remarkably different than what anyone is used to seeing.

As the Holy Spirit transforms us from the inside out, we can bring joy and peace to the world.

Pause & Reflect

Take a moment to reflect on what you just read and what the Holy Spirit is revealing to you today.

- What physical indications of stress—increased heart rate, muscle tension, stomach aches, etc.—have I experienced when thinking about my finances?
- How has anxiety about finances crept into my relationships?
- What would it do for my physical, emotional, mental and spiritual health to experience the joy and peace of Christ?
- What resources or support do I need to seek out in my journey of surrender?

_____

_____

_____

_____

_____

_____

_____

_____

_____

_____

_____

_____

_____

Prayer of Surrender

Spirit of God,

You are the source of life and blessing. It is only through you that I can bear good fruit that lasts. Therefore, I surrender myself to you today.

Specifically, I ask for freedom from any anxiety and depression that money is causing me. May your joy and peace be evidenced in my financial decisions today and throughout this week.

Prompt me when my decisions are not in step with your perfect design. You can always be trusted, so I will follow you today.

In Jesus's name I pray,

Amen.

Peace in the Basement
Story of Surrender: Susan

"God, why is this happening again?" she sobbed. "I can't do this anymore!"

Susan remembers this prayer of desperation at her lowest point in a financial journey marked by twists, turns and too many disappointments to number.

Nearly five years earlier, she and her husband, Tom, believed they could finally fulfill their dream of her being a stay-at-home mom. Between the success of Tom's new business and their intention to downsize, they felt financially secure enough for her to quit her full-time position. As an extra measure of caution, they planned to move into her parents' basement for a short-time—six months tops—while they saved for a down payment on a more affordable home.

Susan and Tom could not have foreseen all the obstacles they would face in the months and years that followed. The unexpected blessing of a third child. A failed home inspection. Growing ethical concerns about the decisions that Tom's partners were making, prompting him to step away from the business. Three times they were ready to buy a home, only to be thwarted by a new major wrench in their plans.

"My parents are great, amazing people and they have a beautiful home," says Susan, "but that is *not* where we wanted to be."

Finally, four years into their basement residency, they were ready to make a purchase—until their lender called about an issue with their credit. Just a week before closing, they discovered Tom's old partners had continued to rack up business expenses on a credit card that was issued in his name. They had stopped making any payments, and Tom was on the hook for $50,000 in debt.

"It was devastating," says Susan. "There was a lot of hurt and anger that people could do this to you. And we had no control over the situation."

At the end of her own strength, Susan did the only thing she knew to do.

"I just started praying my go-to verse when I'm worried or unsure," she says. "'Don't worry about anything. Instead pray about everything, tell God what you need and thank him for all He has done. Then you will experience God's peace.'" (Philippians 4:6-7, paraphrased).

Susan says the peace that washed over her in that moment is unexplainable.

"I felt instantaneous peace over that situation," she remembers. "I didn't know what was going to happen; I just knew He had it under control."

In the days and months that followed, Susan and Tom saw God move mountains that had previously felt insurmountable. Five years into their waiting, they moved into a beautiful home, in a neighborhood they now view as the epicenter of God's mission for them.

"God brought us here, and I think it was as much about His love for our neighbors as it was about us," she says. "He has given us countless opportunities to minister to hurting people on this block. We could have lived anywhere, but this is the time and place where He has called us to be a light."

"It's not always easy to find peace and joy in the middle of God's plan," she continues, "but He's always got something better for us than what we can see in those moments. And the more times you go through situations like this, the easier it is to look back and see His faithfulness."

"Regardless of my circumstances, I can have peace knowing that God's got this," concludes Susan. "I don't have to know the plan to understand that He's working it all together for my good."

Watch and Learn

Watch the video titled, "Joy and Peace" found at MoneySpirit.org for further teaching and reflection.

Notes

1. Connolly, Maureen, and Slade, Margot. "The United States of Stress 2019." Everyday Health. Oct. 23, 2018. www.everydayhealth.com/wellness/united-states-of-stress/

2. Thielen, Paula. "The Connection Between Financial Well-Being and Mental Health." *Forbes*. March 14, 2023. www.forbes.com/sites/forbesfinancecouncil/2023/03/14/the-connection-between-financial-well-being-and-mental-health

3. Swalm, Emily. "Money Anxiety is Common, But You Don't Have to Handle it Alone"

4. National Council for Mental Wellbeing, The Importance of Practicing Gratitude and Celebrating Small Victories

Chapter 4
Patience and Self-Control

> *I know what it is to be in need, and I know what it is to have plenty. I have learned the secret of being content in any and every situation, whether well-fed or hungry, whether living in plenty or in want. I can do all this through him who gives me strength.*
> **Philippians 4:12-13**

Recently, I reached into the fridge for a prepackaged protein drink for my morning commute. This is my standard, daily cuisine—not because I love it, but because in my 40s, I've yet to manage my time wisely enough for a sit-and-enjoy breakfast.

Hurry. Hurry. Hurry.

Rush. Rush. Rush.

That's the steady pace of my current life and the source of so many personal struggles—more than I care to elaborate on in this book. Anyway...

My typical breakfast that morning was anything but. *Um—why is this warm?*

I touched the neighboring gallon of milk. *Warm.*

The tub of margarine. *Warm.*

The wall of the fridge. *Warm.*

I pulled out the freezer drawer, and much to my chagrin, I discovered bloody meat, floppy pizzas and an assortment of stray vegetables floating leisurely around the bottom.

Ugh.... The day we'd long anticipated had finally arrived. Our trusty fridge had breathed its final, frosty breath.

Fast forward a few hours: my husband and I went on an exciting date to Lowe's Home Improvement. They were having their semi-annual blow-out sale on all major kitchen appliances.

What a miraculous coincidence, right?! It certainly felt that way.

You see, our refrigerator is not the only kitchen appliance that's been showing its age-related wear-and-tear these days. In fact, we have a dishwasher and stove that are … how shall I put this? … janky.

Yes, our dishwasher gets our dishes clean (mostly), but only after a minor wrestling match to load it. My husband jerry-rigged the bottom rack several months ago to "sort-of" slide after four of the six roller wheels fell off and melted against the heating coil. It's functional, but frustrating.

And then there's the stove.

We were ecstatic when the prior owners left this gem behind when we first moved into our home. What we didn't realize is that they had shoved a piece of tinfoil into one of the knobs, which (shockingly) didn't hold up over time. For a while, we used pliers to turn on the gas, but somehow that felt less than safe. So now, we just have one less burner.

All this to say, the package appliance deals at Lowe's seemed particularly providential that evening. Not only could we replace our fridge, but we could replace the *entire* kitchen suite in one fell swoop!

A new fridge, dishwasher and stove would match. New appliances would make our lives so much easier. New appliances would have exciting new features that we'd never even realized we wanted.

We *deserved* these appliances! We *needed* these appliances! And all of it could be ours—for zero down and 12 months of easy, interest-free payments.

Thankfully, we had the sense to hold off on making a knee-jerk decision. We wanted to sleep on it, and yes, to pray on it.

Morning came, and the Holy Spirit coupled with a good night of sleep made it crystal clear. *Lord, help us!* We didn't *need* all those things. This was *exactly* the kind of problematic greed we've surrendered—time and time again!

Our ancient stove and wonky dishwasher are annoying, but they are, in fact, no big deal. My "problem" appliances are the very definition of #firstworldproblems.

We dipped into our emergency savings to get a reasonably priced fridge. Everything else can wait.

One of Everything, Please!

Perhaps more than any others, the Spiritual fruits of patience (or "forbearance," as the NIV calls it) and self-control run in stark contrast to the values of this world. We want a little bit of *everything*, and we want it *now!*

When it comes to our finances, the fallout from this collective greed and haste is pervasive.

- We want instant gratification, so we buy on credit and rack up lots of debt.
- We spend beyond our means—and, again, rack up lots of debt.
- We don't bother saving, so we're not prepared for financial emergencies.
- On top of that, we've got nothing set aside for the future.
- And since we don't even want to think about learning patience or self-control, we just stick our heads in the sand and ignore our finances. This only makes our problems worse!

There's no getting around it—the fruit of impatience, self-indulgence and neglect will always taste bitter.

> The fruit of impatience, self-indulgence and neglect will always taste bitter.

There Must Be a Better Way

There is a far better way, and it starts with surrendering to Jesus.

Paul describes it this way: "I have learned the secret of being content in any and every situation, whether well fed or hungry, whether living in plenty or in want. I can do all this through him who gives me strength." (Philippians 4:12b-13)

So how exactly does one experience this kind of surrendered contentment?

1. Recognize the conflict.

We cannot, as so many would suggest, "follow our hearts," because, in our flesh, we will always lean toward greed and instant gratification.

The world says, "If it feels good, do it." and "If you want it, get it." That's not, however, what the Spirit says. In fact, the Spirit equates this kind of self-gratification with idolatry (see Colossians 3:5).

Just because it "feels right" in the moment doesn't mean that it is.

*"For the flesh desires what is contrary to the Spirit, and the Spirit what is contrary to the flesh. They are in conflict with each other, so that **you are not to do whatever you want**."* (Galatians 5:17, emphasis added.)

2. Put sinful desires to death.

Patience and self-control are not passively acquired. Rather, they require an active, definitive decision to turn away from our human instincts and follow God's leading instead.

Paul writes, *"Those who belong to Christ Jesus have crucified the flesh."* (Galatians 5:24a)

As one commentator put it, "We all have evil desires, and we can't ignore them. In order for us to follow the Holy Spirit's guidance, we must deal with them decisively (crucify them)."[1]

Depending on the source of your temptations, that might mean steering clear of those places and situations where the flesh is weak—such as uninstalling the Amazon app on your phone, cutting up your credit cards, or avoiding Lowe's during their semi-annual appliance sales.

> When we put our sinful nature to death, we create space and opportunity for the Spirit to raise us to new life.

The good news? When we put our sinful nature to death, we create space and opportunity for the Spirit to raise us to new life.

> *"And if the Spirit of him who raised Jesus from the dead is living in you, he who raised Christ from the dead will also give life to your mortal bodies because of his Spirit who lives in you. ... For if you live according to the flesh, you will die; but if by the Spirit you put to death the misdeeds of the body, you will live."* (Romans 8:11,13)

3. Listen to the Spirit.

Surrendering to the work of the Holy Spirit is not unlike any other relationship. It takes intentionality, and it takes effort. After all, the world will take every moment of your day, every day of the week, if you allow it.

Carve out time, and remove all the distractions. Start small if you need to, then work up to more and more alone time with Him as you grow.

To experience the Holy Spirit's leading, you must make time to sit, listen, watch, worship and pray.

4. Do what the Spirit says.

Finally, in James, we are reminded that hearing God's voice is not enough. We must, in fact, obey Him if we want to experience the blessing.

"Do not merely listen to the word, and so deceive yourselves. Do what it says. ... But whoever looks intently into the perfect law that gives freedom, and continues in it— not forgetting what they have heard, but doing it—they will be blessed in what they do." (James 1:22, 25)

Worth the Wait

As we are transformed from the inside, the fruit of patience and self-control will change every aspect of how we manage money:

- We'll live in contentment, only buying things we can afford.
- We won't take on unnecessary debt that will only weigh us down.
- We'll live with boundaries in place.
- We'll save a portion of our income, preparing for unforeseen bumps in the road.
- We won't be afraid to examine our finances, because we want to be a faithful steward of all that God has given to us.

God is good, and He wants His children to live in freedom. But to experience that freedom, we have to be willing to rest in Him, trust in His provision, and submit to His control.

So how about it? Do you want to experience the sweet goodness of what God can do in your finances?

Don't settle for a rushed and bitter alternative. Good fruit is always worth the wait.

Pause & Reflect

Take a moment to reflect on what you just read and what the Holy Spirit is revealing to you today.

- What excuses have I made to justify rash or reckless financial decisions?
- In what type of situations am I most tempted to overspend?
- What kind of boundaries or support should I put in place to avoid that kind of temptation?
- How can I carve out more time and space to listen for the voice of the Holy Spirit?

_____

_____

_____

_____

_____

_____

_____

_____

_____

_____

_____

_____

_____

Prayer of Surrender

Spirit of God,

You are the source of life and blessing. It is only through you that I can bear good fruit that lasts. Therefore, I surrender myself to you today.

Specifically, I submit to your good and perfect boundaries. May your patience and self-control be evidenced in my financial decisions today and throughout this week.

Prompt me when my decisions are not in step with your perfect design. You can always be trusted, so I will follow you today.

In Jesus's name I pray,

Amen.

"God, Show Us a Way"
Story of Surrender: Willie and Tina

While students in college, Willie and Tina made big plans together. Their first one was to get married, so they got engaged. After that, each intended to pursue the careers for which they had both been training—Willie in criminal justice and Tina as a lawyer.

According to their dream scenario, the couple imagined a financially secure future. Instead, they found themselves with fluctuating income levels, sky-rocketing expenses and loads of student debt.

Upon graduation, Willie found work in law enforcement and Tina continued into law school. After receiving her law degree, Tina discovered that finding a foothold in the law field wasn't as easy as promised. "You don't necessarily get the job they sell you on," she explains.

To increase opportunity, the couple moved to a larger, metropolitan area but soon experienced culture shock. Expenses were double compared to where they had been living!

To make ends meet, Tina opted for a loan deferral which allowed her to stop paying one loan to pay for another. What wasn't made clear, however, was that the deferred loan would continue to compound interest during the deferral period.

"By the time you realize what's happening" exclaims Tina, "you owe more than you did on the day you graduated!"

Determined to keep their personal finances tied to their trust in God, Willie and Tina resolved to meet their financial challenges as good stewards. But this would take some time, especially getting on the same page about money.

"My background is: once money hit my pocket, it was gone," says Willie. "Tina's family was different. They were very much into saving, tithing and giving to ministry. "

The couple began with prayer, asking simply and directly, "God, show us a way to become debt-free."

This meant driving past favorite restaurants on Sundays after attending worship services at their church. It meant squashing ideas about taking a trip to celebrate their wedding anniversary. It meant deciding that three pairs of black shoes were enough, no matter the doorbuster price on a fourth pair!

"If you want to live a life that is free-flowing, where you are not living paycheck to paycheck, you need self-control," adds Tina.

Also, saving and investing became important means for bringing down debt. When unexpected expenses caught the couple by surprise, they sold stock or withdrew from their savings to pay it off.

"This came from learning how to be better stewards," notes Willie. "We became investors of our money, instead of just spenders."

Even while paying down debt, Willie and Tina maintained their priorities of tithing and giving.

"When I was working hourly," recalls Tina "I would look at my hours even before I got my paycheck, to see what my tithe would be. Anything I gave over that was my offering."

While steadily applying patience and self-control, the couple eventually managed to significantly pay down their debt.

"God made a way where I became free from accumulated credit card debt, and we paid off $70K of student debt," exclaims Tina. "Our credit card score was never higher!"

Willie and Tina are grateful to have realized a plan they hadn't dreamed up together in college.

"We got to a point where we were side-by-side, taking care of bills, taking care of investments, understanding more about how to make your money make money for you, and still be a blessing to others," recalls Willie.

"We became spiritual fiduciaries," adds Willie. "God has blessed us, but we also have this responsibility to be good stewards."

Watch and Learn

Watch the video titled, "Patience and Self-Control" found at MoneySpirit.org for further teaching and reflection.

Notes

1. *Life Application Bible: New International Version*. Grand Rapids, MI: Zondervan; Carol Stream, IL: Tyndale, 2011. Print. [Notes on Galatians 5:24]

Chapter 5
Kindness and Gentleness

Therefore, as God's chosen people, holy and dearly loved, clothe yourselves with compassion, kindness, humility, gentleness and patience.

Colossians 3:12

Recently, I visited a neighborhood on the south side of Chicago known as Roseland. It's one of the most impoverished communities in the city, let alone the country. From the outside looking in, Roseland is an urban wasteland of graffiti, iron-gated windows and makeshift beds of cardboard and dirty blankets.

But it hasn't always been this way.

In fact, the very name of the neighborhood comes from the beautiful flowers that once lined the bustling, well-manicured streets—including the south end of Chicago's famed Michigan Avenue. European immigrants, skilled tradesmen and aspiring businessmen once flocked to the cosmopolitan area where they could find any number of lucrative jobs, such as in the booming steel industry or at George M. Pullman's nearby luxury railcar factory.

The winds of change began to blow, however, as industry trends led to the shutdown of steel mills, local factories and, eventually, Pullman's production facilities. Meanwhile, an influx of African Americans led to widespread fear-mongering and corrupt real estate practices. During this mass period of "white flight," light-skinned families moved to the suburbs, taking their businesses, influence and dollars with them.

Over time, the place once known for beauty and bounty developed a new reputation for economic devastation, violent racial riots and crime.

Roseland's story is one of abandonment, lost opportunity and oppression. Yet in the middle of the neighborhood is a small church attempting to write a different story.

Roseland Christian Ministries invites all members of the neighborhood to "come as you are." They "provide places where all are welcome and programs that care for the physical, emotional and spiritual needs of Chicago's Roseland community."[1]

The day of my visit, I was touched by the thousands of different ways their small staff and an army of volunteers are sharing the love and kindness of Christ to their community. Their compassion is truly remarkable!

They provide warm meals, hot showers, laundry services and so much more for anyone in need. They also house several mothers and their children—without question or condition—who need a safe and comfortable place to stay. There are no restrictions on how long women can reside in the shelter. Some stay a few weeks; others stay well beyond a year.

"We want this to be their final shelter," Kadie, the shelter's director shared with me. "That means giving them the time, resources and space they need to get back on their feet."

"When they come to us, they're in the middle of trauma," she continued. "They aren't in a place to hear the gospel, so we show it to them instead. We just love them as Jesus loves us. It takes time to build trust and relationships. Then we can have those conversations."

The result of this ministry is a beautiful picture of the Kingdom of God.

On Sunday mornings, the church's pews are filled with those who have been victims of poverty, abandonment, addictions, homelessness and, in some cases, fatal crimes against their loved ones. Sitting by their sides are descendants of families who once fled the area out of fear.

Together, the restored lift their voices in boisterous praise songs of hope, joy and faith—and they are eager to welcome anyone and everyone who wants to join them. Every Sunday and throughout the week that follows, they serve alongside each other, loving their neighborhood as Jesus would.

They are joint benefactors and carriers of the Holy Spirit's gifts of kindness and gentleness.

What the Goats Are Doing

When it comes to our finances, showing kindness and gentleness may provide the greatest opportunity to reflect God's heart toward others. Why is that? Because God's fruit is so strikingly different than the world's.

To the world, money is:

- A means of power and control. The more we gain, the more status and influence we have.
- A weapon. We give or withhold it to maintain power over other people.
- How we improve our position in life—even if it means taking advantage of others.
- Something we have earned because we are hardworking and worthy.
- Something only to be given when we can measure the ROI, receive goods or services in return or expect repayment with interest.

That fruit, my friends, is rotten.

In God's kingdom, however, money is a tool we use to bless the lives of others. It's used to restore what has been lost and to elevate those who have been beaten down by the weight of this world.

> In God's kingdom, money is a tool we use to bless the lives of others.

Not because they've earned it.

Not because they've proven they can be trusted.

Not because we have *any* idea how our situation or theirs will (or won't) improve.

In God's kingdom, we give because *God* prompts us to give in response to the very real and present needs around us. When the Holy Spirit moves us, we give our money freely and without condition, knowing it was never really *our* money to control in the first place.

In Matthew 25:31-46, Jesus speaks very plainly about this financial responsibility.

> *"When the Son of Man comes in his glory, and all the angels with him, he will sit on his glorious throne. All the nations will be gathered before him, and he will separate the people one from another as a shepherd separates the sheep from the goats. He will put the sheep on his right and the goats on his left.*
>
> *"Then the King will say to those on his right, 'Come, you who are blessed by my Father; take your inheritance, the kingdom prepared for you since the creation of the world. For I was hungry and you gave me something to eat, I was thirsty and you gave me some-*

thing to drink, I was a stranger and you invited me in, I needed clothes and you clothed me, I was sick and you looked after me, I was in prison and you came to visit me.'

"Then the righteous will answer him, 'Lord, when did we see you hungry and feed you, or thirsty and give you something to drink? When did we see you a stranger and invite you in, or needing clothes and clothe you? When did we see you sick or in prison and go to visit you?'

"The King will reply, 'Truly I tell you, whatever you did for one of the least of these brothers and sisters of mine, you did for me.'

"Then he will say to those on his left, 'Depart from me, you who are cursed, into the eternal fire prepared for the devil and his angels. For I was hungry and you gave me nothing to eat, I was thirsty and you gave me nothing to drink, I was a stranger and you did not

invite me in, I needed clothes and you did not clothe me, I was sick and in prison and you did not look after me.'

"They also will answer, 'Lord, when did we see you hungry or thirsty or a stranger or needing clothes or sick or in prison, and did not help you?'

"He will reply, 'Truly I tell you, whatever you did not do for one of the least of these, you did not do for me.'

"Then they will go away to eternal punishment, but the righteous to eternal life."

> **When the Holy Spirit prompts them, God's sheep give with open hands and open hearts.**

To be clear, if the voice inside your head is rationalizing disregard for those who are hungry, thirsty or imprisoned, it's not the Shepherd talking. So don't be a goat!

When the Holy Spirit prompts them, God's sheep give with open hands and open hearts.

On Earth as it is in Heaven

You see, in God's kingdom, kindness and gentleness aren't rare occurrences; they're a way of life—because God is kind and gentle. They're not just nice ideas; they bring the kingdom of God to earth, right here where we are.

Do you remember when Jesus taught His disciples to pray? His model prayer included the desire that God's will be done *"on earth as it is in heaven."* (see Matthew 6:10).

When we walk in step with Jesus, we are aware of the needs around us. We share our resources freely, without expecting anything in return. We give sacrificially when God asks us to, because we trust Him to provide the means.

And because we understand God sometimes uses other people to answer *our* prayers, we receive financial blessings from others without guilt. We gracefully accept the kindness and gentleness of God's people with gratitude.

For many of us, this is the harder lesson to learn. Perhaps it's easy for you to put cash *in* the giving box, but it is an entirely different experience to *receive* financial support when you need it.

Pride can be a hard pill to swallow, especially when it comes to money.

Whether it's $2 or $2,000, self-sufficient people are often quick to shoo away help that might make them seem anything less than hardworking, independent and in control.

> **Pride can be a hard pill to swallow, especially when it comes to money.**

"I'm not a charity case."

"I don't need anyone's help."

"Give your money to someone who needs it more than me."

These are all phrases that might indicate a prideful heart that's become hardened against the kindness and gentleness of a loving Father.

Perhaps God wants to provide for you in unexpected ways. Perhaps when you turn away generosity, you are stealing blessings from God's people who have been moved by the Holy Spirit to give in *your* time of need.

Humbly accepting the gift, saying "thank you" and praising the Father for His provision might be exactly what you need to experience "thy Kingdom come" in your life and circumstances today.

Blooming Where You're Planted

So where do you find yourself today?

Do you see money only as a way to achieve personal gain?

Or is money a tool you are willing to give and receive for something so much greater than yourself?

Jesus invites you to daily surrender, and His Spirit can fill you with kindness and gentleness if you let Him.

As you reflect God's fruit in your finances, you will help advance His Kingdom right here where you're planted.

Pause & Reflect

Take a moment to reflect on what you just read and what the Holy Spirit is revealing to you today.

- Re-read the examples of how the world views money on page 77. Where have I seen evidence of this "rotten" fruit in my own life?
- How might God want me to show His gentleness and kindness to the world with the money He's entrusted to me?
- In what ways has pride or control robbed me of openly giving and receiving God's blessings?

_____

_____

_____

_____

_____

_____

_____

_____

_____

Prayer of Surrender

Spirit of God,

You are the source of life and blessing. It is only through you that I can bear good fruit that lasts. Therefore, I surrender myself to you today.

Specifically, I ask that You rid me of any pride or illusions of control that get in the way of giving and receiving Your blessings. May your kindness and gentleness be evidenced in my financial decisions today and throughout this week.

Prompt me when my decisions are not in step with your perfect design. You can always be trusted, so I will follow you today.

In Jesus's name I pray,

Amen.

It Changes Everything
Story of Surrender: Joe and Sue

"I wouldn't be here if it wasn't for God's kindness," says Joe, visibly moved by the memories.

Though he was first saved at the age of 19, it would be 20 more years—and well into his marriage with Sue—before he would escape the bondage of drug and alcohol addictions.

"I wanted to change my life, but I didn't know how," says Joe.

Sue says God used the kindness of His people to help sustain her through those years.

"A lot of people stepped in to meet our physical needs at the time," she says, "but mostly it was just their prayers and their words of encouragement. I got to a point where I didn't love him anymore. I had a friend say, 'I'm going to pray that you love him like the way that you met him, that very first day.'"

"Honestly, I didn't think it would work," she continues. "Then one day, I just felt like the Lord said to me, 'You need to see him the way I see him.' That just totally blew my mind! It changed everything."

"She loved me the way only God could," remembers Joe. "Finally, I just had to surrender. I fell to my knees at home, and I just said, 'Lord, I've got to do this.' And I quit everything cold turkey."

These days, Joe owns a successful business, and he serves as a deacon for the church where he and Sue are actively involved. Not only do they give their first fruits to the church's ministry, but they're quick to lend a hand or donate financially, whenever and wherever they see a need.

"We feel called to be 'first responders,'" explains Joe. "Anytime somebody needs something, we want to be able to write a check or give of our time. Everything I have is because of Him. As long as He continues to open up the doors, we'll just keep giving.'"

Together, they are committed to sharing God's kindness to everyone, because they've seen the power of it firsthand.

"If we can just continue to look at people the way God looks at them, it makes all the difference in the world," says Sue. "The true love of Christ really changes people. I'm a living testimony of that."

Watch and Learn

Watch the video titled, "Kindness and Gentleness" found at MoneySpirit.org for further teaching and reflection.

Notes

1. Roseland Christian Ministries. roselandchristianministries.org. Accessed March 7, 2024.

Chapter 6
Faithfulness and Goodness

> *By their fruit you will recognize them. Do people pick grapes from thorn bushes, or figs from thistles? Likewise, every good tree bears good fruit, but a bad tree bears bad fruit.*
>
> **Matthew 7:16-17**

At 17 years old, I had the incredible opportunity to travel to Moscow on a work-and-witness trip with my church. Besides me, the group included one other teenage girl—let's call her Phoebe—and about a dozen older, wiser, very capable adults.

I mention the group's makeup because, for the life of me, I still don't understand why Phoebe and I received the assignment that we did. On the first working day of our trip, we were handed hammers, nails and a stack of thin, wooden planks.

"What you're going to do," our leader told us, as he walked us into a simple, bare-bones room, "is nail these boards vertically along that wall. Take your time. There's a ladder you can use."

With that, he left us alone to interpret and execute his straightforward instructions.

Now here's the thing…

I'm all for gender equality and the empowerment of young girls. I know many ladies, young and old, who can wield a power tool like nobody's business. Many women excel in construction-related tasks.

But we were not among them.

In fact, I'm not even sure Phoebe or I had held a hammer before that day.

Perhaps even worse, we didn't even have the sense to realize we didn't know what we were doing. We happily climbed up and down the ladder, chit-chatting and laughing as together we did the Lord's work.

The first plank went up smoothly. We missed the nails more often than we hit them, but the end result was a board solidly secured to the wall. Nice! High fives all around.

Phoebe and I lined up the next board right beside it. Nailed it! (literally) And then the next, and then the next, and then the next one after that.

Eventually, we stood back to admire our work…only to realize something had gone terribly wrong.

The second board was just a hair—barely even visible—angled to the right. The next leaned a smidge more off-center. Each sequential board slanted a little further, like sunflowers reaching and bowing toward the light.

Tilting our heads and squinting, it didn't seem *so* bad. "*Think they'll notice?*" we wondered aloud.

They did. They absolutely did.

I learned three important lessons that day…

1. Confidence is great. Skilled and informed confidence is better.
2. It's deflating—not to mention time-consuming—to rip everything down and start completely over.
3. There's this cool thing called a "plumb line," and it makes all the difference when you're paneling a wall.

With the patience of Job, our leader showed us how we could hang a string above our workspace with a screw tied to the bottom of it. Gravity would pull the string perpendicular to the ground. So long as we consistently measured our boards according to the plumb line, we could be confident in the vertical integrity of our wall.

Armed with our handy-dandy plumb line, coupled with close adult supervision/assistance and ample time, we eventually celebrated an appropriately completed project.

Out-of-Line Behaviors

It didn't take a master carpenter to recognize the depths of our teenage ignorance.

Likewise, it's usually not hard to spot the bad fruit when our financial thoughts and behaviors have gotten out of line.

Secrets. Lies. Deception. Corruption. Rash behavior. Shame.

In Matthew chapter 7, Jesus explains a sure-fire way to spot those who are disconnected from the Father. He says, "*By their fruit, you will recognize them. Are grapes gathered from thornbushes, or figs from thistles? Likewise, every good tree bears good fruit, but a bad tree bears bad fruit.*" (Matthew 7:16-17).

Ok, but what exactly constitutes "good"—and when it comes to our finances, what is good *enough*?

It's tempting to define the answer to this question by the world's standards or in comparison to our peers.

It's not like I'm doing anything illegal.

At least I'm not as reckless as her.

I certainly put more into the offering plate than they do.

I'm not hurting anybody—and nobody is ever going to know.

Everybody does it! What's the big deal?!

Truth is, there is no such thing as "good enough." Comparisons mean nothing in God's kingdom. We are called to a higher standard.

The plumb line is *God's* goodness. Anything that veers to the left or the right is bad.

But how can we *possibly* live by that standard? Left on our own, we've all got a little lean in our walk.

By now you surely know the answer: we stay connected to the Father, daily surrendering to the Spirit's control.

> The plumb line is God's goodness. Anything that veers to the left or the right is bad.

"*Whoever sows to please their flesh, from the flesh will reap destruction; whoever sows to please the Spirit, from the*

Spirit will reap eternal life. Let us not become weary in doing good, for at the proper time we will reap a harvest if we do not give up." (Galatians 6:8-9)

This "not giving up" requires daily, faithful, intentional decisions to follow the promptings of the Holy Spirit, in every decision, big AND small.

In her book *Surrender: The Heart God Controls*, author Nancy DeMoss Wolgemuth writes,

"Our initial surrender to Christ was the launching pad for a lifetime of continual surrender and sacrifice. Now, on a daily, perpetual basis, we are called to live out that consecration, by responding to the various circumstances and choices of life in obedience and surrendering to His will."[1]

As we already know, everything we have belongs to God—our money, our possessions, our, well… everything. We're not the owners; we're managers of *His* resources that have been entrusted to us.

As managers of God's resources, obedience to Jesus is everything.

So, it's only natural that we surrender it back to His control. As we hand over that control, the Holy Spirit will sow goodness and faithfulness into the ways we view and manage God's money.

As managers of God's resources, obedience to Jesus is everything. His priorities are our priorities. His Word is our guide. We trust in His provision, and we faithfully follow His leading. We set aside our first fruits—our best fruits—for Him, and when He asks us to give more, we joyfully do.

And since we know it's not *really* our money, we quit being careless or wasteful. We seek out wise counsel, and we are diligent in our saving, our spending and our investing.

Gone are the days when we thought it was okay to cheat a little bit here, or lie a little bit there, in order to get ahead. Instead, we practice integrity in all our financial dealings.

Jesus calls the shots when it comes to our money, and we are happy to obey.

Sometimes that means a minor course correction as we recognize we're leaning away from the plumb line. Other times, that means ripping it all down and starting over. It might also mean pursuing forgiveness and restoration with those we've hurt along the way.

Crooked finances can't be left alone.

No more cutting corners, no more get-rich-quick schemes. Jesus calls the shots when it comes to our money, and we are happy to obey.

As the seeds of faithfulness and goodness begin to take root in our souls, the quality of His spiritual fruit will be unmistakable.

We will taste and see that the Lord is good, and we'll be able to introduce others to the sweetness of walking and abiding in Him.

Pause & Reflect

Take a moment to reflect on what you just read and what the Holy Spirit is revealing to you today.

- When it comes to my finances, where have I been most tempted to cut corners, bend the truth, waste, cheat, steal or lie?
- In comparison to the plumb line of God's goodness and God's faithfulness, where are my finances out-of-line?
- Are there any crooked areas where I need to rip it down, repair and/or restore?

Prayer of Surrender

Spirit of God,

You are the source of life and blessing. It is only through you that I can bear good fruit that lasts. Therefore, I surrender myself to you today.

Specifically, I ask that you reveal any areas where my finances are out-of-line with what you want to do in and through me. May your goodness and faithfulness be evidenced in my financial decisions today and throughout this week.

Prompt me when my decisions are not in step with your perfect design. You can always be trusted, so I will follow you today.

In Jesus's name I pray,

Amen.

Defining the Ground Rules
Story of Surrender: Philip and Rachel

Two methodical people, Philip and Rachel have never been ones to make rash decisions. So, when they decided to buy their first home as a married couple, they took their time and carefully weighed the options.

"We bought a townhome for less than what we would have been pre-approved for, and we made sure we could totally cover the cost," recalls Rachel. "We also prayed about it and sought the wisdom of others. The conventional wisdom at the time was that you can't go wrong buying a house."

That, as Rachel describes it, turned out to be "catastrophically wrong." Six months after moving in, the bottom dropped out on the housing market.

"We bought at exactly the wrong time," explains Philip.

Even so, Philip and Rachel remember being happy in their townhome for the first year or so. The recession felt far away and disconnected from their daily lives. By the second year there, however, they saw all kinds of troubling signs around them.

Neighbors were moving out in the middle of the night. An entire row of buildings was left half-finished. Identical homes down the street were sitting unsold, priced for 50 to 60 percent less than what they'd purchased theirs.

Over time, and especially once their daughter entered the picture, the need to relocate became increasingly clear. They needed childcare, and

Rachel had taken a job 30 miles south, near family in their hometown.

Selling—even through a short sale—seemed virtually impossible, and they wanted to avoid foreclosure. They turned to a legal advisor who told them about a third option: deed in lieu of foreclosure. The stakes were high; if the bank didn't go for it, they could face bankruptcy. However, after countless prayers and consulting with advisors, they determined it was their only path forward.

As they dove into the arduous process, Philip and Rachel outlined a few ground rules they each would follow.

"No matter what, we were going to be totally honest," says Philip. "We were not going to hide or withhold information—which frankly, our lawyer encouraged us to do. Secondly, we decided that no matter what they would throw at us, we were going to be as kind and understanding as we could possibly be."

"We also had a rule that we weren't going to let this affect our marriage," adds Rachel. "We were a team, and no matter what, we'd carry this weight together."

These rules turned out to be far more difficult to keep than what they had imagined.

Whenever they called their mortgage company, the person on the other end of the line always had an agenda. Whether it was through lies, threats or even name-calling and yelling at times, he did everything in his power to make them question their decision.

"It was his job to be antagonistic," remembers Philip. "Maintaining a sense of decorum was hard."

"We took turns making calls so we could give each other a break," adds Rachel. "It was very intense and stressful."

One day, Philip received a phone call informing him the battle was suddenly over.

"I was driving home from work, and I had to pull over to process what he was saying," says Philip. "It was finally clear. There was this incredible sense of relief."

Philip and Rachel are quick to clarify that they didn't come out of their housing ordeal unscathed. Their credit score took a hit, and they still had payments to make. However, as they surrendered their situation to Christ, they experienced His strength and presence all along the way.

"We felt God's hand was moving in all of this," says Philip.

"We tried to be representatives of Christ in this horrible situation, as best as we could," says Rachel. "And even though we had consequences, it still felt like God was Master of the whole thing."

"I just kept thinking about the verse: "What good is it for someone to gain the whole world, yet forfeit their soul?" she summarizes.2 "Our circumstances can strip us of things, but they don't have to strip us of who we are and where we find our meaning."

Watch and Learn

Watch the video titled, "Faithfulness and Goodness" found at MoneySpirit.org for further teaching and reflection.

Notes:

1. DeMoss Wolgemuth, Nancy. *Surrender: The Heart God Controls*. Chicago, IL. Moody Publishers. 2005.
2. See Mark 8:36.

Chapter 7
What's Your Story?

> *"You are the light of the world. A town built on a hill cannot be hidden. Neither do people light a lamp and put it under a bowl. Instead they put it on its stand, and it gives light to everyone in the house. In the same way, let your light shine before others, that they may see your good deeds and glorify your Father in heaven."*
>
> **Matthew 5:14**

Throughout the pages of this book, you've read story after story of the sweet fruit that is produced when we fully surrender our finances to the work of the Holy Spirit.

You've read some of my personal journey. You've also read snippets from friends and acquaintances who were vulnerable enough to share how they've seen God at work through their money.

In these stories, I pray you have seen glimpses of your own struggles and that you have been encouraged that change *is* possible. The same God who brought joy, peace, love and so much more into these "stories of surrender" can do amazing things for you if you allow Him.

Truth be told, however, this was one of the biggest challenges of writing this book: finding people willing to share their testimonies.

I don't, for one second, believe this is because stories of financial restoration are rare. In fact, I know many, many people who have firsthand experience with the transformative power of the Holy Spirit.

- They've traded fleeting prestige for the unconditional love of the Father.
- They've found joy, peace and contentment with what they have been given.
- They've learned self-control in establishing God-honoring boundaries.
- They've given to others abundantly, meeting the very real needs of those around them.

- They've quit cheating the system and cutting corners, pursuing financial integrity instead.
- They've trusted God with everything, and in everything, He's proven faithful.

So, what gives? Why are people so reticent to share their experiences with others?

Once again, I see this as a symptom of a truth that we've already uncovered: Talking about money is considered taboo in the church!

No, Not Me!

In my day job, I occasionally get to write life stories about Spirit-led Christians who are entrusting their God-given resources to the Owner and Provider of it all. Sharing these stories is one of the most powerful ways we can educate and inspire others to go and do likewise.

There is no greater evidence of God at work than the story of a transformed life!

However, I'm often met with reluctance when I first reach out to someone for an interview.

The wording may sound slightly different, but at its root, the hesitations I hear are almost always the same. Perhaps you can relate.

1. "I'm not an expert; I don't really know all that much."

Boy does this fear hit close to home!

When my colleagues and I first started discussing a book for me to write about finances, all my internal insecurity alarm bells started going off. I'm a word person, not a number person—by nature *and* by trade. I feared that if I were to write a book about money, I would suddenly be faced with a barrage of questions to which I do not know the answer.

I do not know what a Roth IRA is, regardless of how many times it's been explained to me. I cannot tell you whether a CD is a good choice for your retirement planning. I thought those were replaced by MP3s in the early 2000s! I'm not sure where exactly I'd go to invest in the stock market. Is that somewhere over by Aldi?

Here's what I do know: The Lord put it on my heart to share my story. I trust He knows what He's doing.

I'm encouraged by the testimony of a blind man Jesus healed, as told in John chapter 9. (For context, the Pharisees were attempting to use him as a pawn to uncover dirt about Jesus.)

"A second time they summoned the man who had been blind. 'Give glory to God by telling the truth,' they said. 'We know this man is a sinner.'

"He replied, 'Whether he is a sinner or not, I don't know. **One thing I do know. I was blind but now I see!'"** (John 9:24-25, emphasis added)

> You don't have to know all the answers for God to use your life's story.

Like the blind man, you don't have to know all the answers for God to use your life's story. Share what you *do* know and point back to the One who gave you sight.

2. "I'm not perfect. I still mess things up."

Again…guilty. I mean, for crying out loud, I nearly replaced my entire kitchen a few weeks ago just because my fridge quit working!

We do ourselves and others a disservice when we assume that we must have it all together before our testimony matters. In reality, there is tremendous value in saying, "I'm still struggling; God's still teaching me. Here's what He's shown me so far."

You haven't yet reached perfection—and that's okay! Neither have I. Our stories are still being written, but we can share the chapters that have been finished so far.

I echo the words of Paul, who expressed gratitude for a very imperfect church in Philippi: *"being confident of this, that he who began a good work in you will carry it on to completion until the day of Christ Jesus."* (Philippians 1:6)

3. "I don't want to offend anyone. Who am I to tell others what to do?"

To this I say: why is talking about money so offensive?!

Jesus talked about money—a lot! If we want to be like Him, why shouldn't we?

Furthermore, I know firsthand how entrapped my husband and I have felt whenever our finances have gotten out of whack. When we try to do things our own way, it always gets messy.

Our stories are still being written, but we can share the chapters that have been finished so far.

When I turn things back over to the Author and Giver of life, however, He brings light into my darkness. Why *wouldn't* I want to share that hope with others?!

As Christ's followers, we each have the honor, joy and responsibility of sharing the Gospel—the whole Gospel—with a lost, hurt and broken world. The Good News is more than Heaven! Jesus wants to redeem us, right here, right now, from anything that keeps us in bondage.

> *"How, then, can they call on the one they have not believed in? And how can they believe in the one of whom they have not heard? And how can they hear without someone preaching to them? And how can anyone preach unless they are sent? As it is written: 'How beautiful are the feet of those who bring good news!'" (Romans 10:14-15)*

4. "I don't have that great of a story. I really haven't done all that much."

Is your testimony average? Fantastic! You'll have an easier time connecting with the average Jane and Joe who need God's intervention just like you.

Are your stories short and basic? Wonderful! You don't need a long, drawn-out saga to share examples of God's redemption in your finances. In fact, it's probably better if you don't. Just be willing to share quick, simple anecdotes about the times when you've experienced God's intervention in your life.

My dad, who just so happens to be my favorite preacher of all time, frequently talked about the "feel, felt, found" conversational method. It's a simple, easy-to-remember way to build trust and connection with our neighbors.

It goes like this:

"*I understand how you feel...*" [Affirm the challenge they are facing, and verbalize your empathy for their situation.]

"*I've felt that way before...*" [Share a related obstacle or circumstance in which you've experienced similar fears, frustrations or discouragement in the past.]

"*Here's what I've found...*" [Describe the ways you experienced God's faithfulness in the midst of your struggle.]

The more you get comfortable using this "feel, felt, found" method, the more you'll find natural opportunities to communicate empathy and hope to friends, loved ones and others who so desperately need it.

One word of caution: In your attempt to build connection, be careful not to minimize another person's situation or overemphasize how alike your circumstances have been.

For example, I know the frustration of throwing away spoiled food and needing to spend money I hadn't budgeted to stock a new fridge. What I have *not* experienced is the fear of wondering where my next meal would come from. To compare my 48-hour inconvenience to someone else's ongoing struggle with poverty would be insulting, at best.

However, I *can...*

- affirm the gravity of their circumstances [feel], and
- confess there have been times in my life where I have felt hopeless and afraid [felt], and
- share what I have seen in my own life and in the lives of so many others. [found]

I've found that God is always faithful. He *"make[s] a way in the wilderness and rivers in the desert."* (Isaiah 43:19) He is the *"God who sees,"* (Genesis 16:13), His *love and mercies never cease* (Lamentations 3:22-23) and *"when I am afraid, I can put my trust in [Him]."* (Psalm 56:3)

Your life's story can and should be a redemptive tale that brings glory to God.

5. "I don't want to make it all about me."

Awesome! It's not about you—so don't make it that way. Your life's story can and should be a redemptive tale that brings glory to God.

Jesus, himself, said that our lives should be a light helping others see the goodness of God.

> *"You are the light of the world. A town built on a hill cannot be hidden. Neither do people light a lamp and put it under a bowl. Instead they put it on its stand, and it gives light to everyone in the house. In the same way, let your light shine before others, that they may see your good deeds and glorify your Father in heaven." (Matthew 5:14)*

Humility is a wonderful attribute. However, don't let the fear of vulnerability or concern about "what will people think?" get in the way of God using your experiences for His redemptive purposes. If the Holy Spirit prompts you to speak, speak. Don't silence the words God wants to say through you.

On the other hand, if the Holy Spirit prompts you to stay quiet, stay quiet. It can be a slippery slope—especially for people-pleasing extroverts like me—to go from testifying to bellowing. Bragging—even humble bragging—focuses all the attention on the wrong target.

How can you tell the difference? Pray for the Holy Spirit's guidance to know when to speak, when to stay silent and when to listen.

David's prayer recorded in Psalm 19:14 provides a wonderful example of this kind of heart check: *"May these words of my mouth and the meditation of my heart be pleasing in your sight, LORD, my Rock and my Redeemer."*

Prepare, Protect, Inspire

Perhaps one of the greatest opportunities we have in sharing God's fruit is through our influence with younger generations.

Whether it's as parents, grandparents, aunts, uncles, Sunday school teachers or simply the caring elders next door, we have endless opportunities to create meaningful ripples of transformation for those who come behind us.

Much of what I believe about surrender came from the ongoing, consistent witness of everyday saints who exemplified that faith and obedience throughout my childhood and early adulthood. I don't take it for granted that I was raised by godly parents, and I was mentored by aunts, uncles and hundreds (if not thousands) of men and women who showed me what it meant to honor God with *everything*, including with their money.

Occasionally those financial lessons came from their words about saving, tithing, giving, sharing. More often, it came from observing their everyday, quiet behaviors that always brought glory to God.

- Providing birthday and Christmas gifts to kids who had nothing.
- Dropping their weekly tithe checks into the offering plate.
- Prayerfully seeking God's direction for financial decisions, big and small.
- Hosting college students who were far away from home for Sunday dinner.
- Driving beat-up cars, wearing worn-out clothing, and living simple, no-frills lives without complaint.
- Trusting God to provide just what they needed, at just the right time.
- Leading businesses with integrity.
- Forfeiting prestige and higher salaries to pursue God's vocational calling.

The list goes on and on. Even (in some cases) decades later, I remember in vivid detail countless living testimonies of spiritual financial surrender. And I am forever grateful.

If you have any influence in the life of a young person—and very few of us don't—God can use your life's story to grow His spiritual fruit in theirs.

Share what you've learned.

Walk out God's truth.

Faithfully live in surrender.

God can and will use your influence to financially prepare, protect and inspire the children who follow your lead.

For the Chapters Ahead

Regardless of where you find yourself in this financial journey—whether you are new to the idea of spiritual surrender or you just need the occasional reminder—God is not through with you yet.

As author and pastor Leighton Ford has said, "God loves us the way we are, but He loves us too much to leave us that way."

No doubt, God has so many new things He wants to reveal to you about surrendering your money to Him. He'll provide you with several opportunities to learn and put those lessons into practice.

What's more, God has provided a Counselor, Advocate, Helper and Comforter to guide you along the way. In His "farewell discourse" (John chapters 14-17) near the end of His earthly ministry, Jesus repeatedly promised His disciples we would never walk alone.

> **God has provided a Counselor, Advocate, Helper and Comforter to guide you along the way.**

For example:

> *"If you love me, keep my commands. And I will ask the Father, and he will give you another advocate to help you and be with you forever—the Spirit of truth. The world cannot accept him, because it neither sees him nor knows him. But you know him, for he lives with you and will be in you. I will not leave you as orphans; I will come to you." (John 14:15-18)*

And…

"All this I have spoken while still with you. But the Advocate, the Holy Spirit, whom the Father will send in my name, will teach you all things and will remind you of everything I have said to you. Peace I leave with you; my peace I give you. I do not give to you as the world gives. Do not let your hearts be troubled and do not be afraid." (John 14:25-27)

And again…

"I have much more to say to you, more than you can now bear. But when he, the Spirit of truth, comes, he will guide you into all the truth. He will not speak on his own; he will speak only what he hears, and he will tell you what is yet to come. He will glorify me because it is from me that he will receive what he will make known to you. All that belongs to the Father is mine. That is why I said the Spirit will receive from me what he

will make known to you." (John 16:12-15)

We don't have to fear the future and whatever financial struggles we might face. If there's one message Jesus wanted us to know as He prepared to leave Earth, it seemed to be this: *You are not alone. Trust Me. I will help you, and I will be with you.*

Your story is still being written.

God's fruit will still grow within you, so long as you remain connected to the Vine.

He wants to do such much more in you and through you. Every. Single. Day.

You can experience financial freedom, now and your whole life through. All it will take is your full, unconditional surrender.

Pause & Reflect

Take a moment to reflect on what you just read and what the Holy Spirit is revealing to you today. Lines are provided below to journal some of your thoughts.

- In what ways have I seen God work in and through my financial surrender?
- Where and with whom might I have opportunities to share what God's done in my life?

- What are my hesitations in sharing my testimony with those who need hope and encouragement? Is it the Spirit directing me to stay silent, or is it my own fears and insecurities?

_____

_____

_____

_____

_____

_____

_____

_____

_____

_____

_____

_____

_____

_____

_____

_____

_____

_____

_____

Prayer of Surrender

Spirit of God,

You are the source of life and blessing. It is only through you that I can bear good fruit that lasts. Therefore, I surrender myself to you today.

Specifically, I surrender my life's story to you. Use me as you wish to encourage, bless and redeem the people around me. May your fruit be evidenced in my financial decisions today and throughout this week.

Prompt me when my decisions are not in step with your perfect design. You can always be trusted, and so I will follow you today.

In Jesus's name I pray,

Amen.

We'd Love to Hear Your Story!

What has the Holy Spirit revealed to you through this study? How are you seeing His fruit in your finances? We'd love to hear from you!

Visit MoneySpirit.org to share your story today.

Money and Spirit
Discussion Guide

While this book can be read alone, it is most effective when studied with a partner or small group.

By joining with a partner or group, you can inspire, encourage and teach one another as God reveals new truths to you, and you can ask each other questions for clearer understanding. You can also hold each other accountable so that you are more likely to build godly, healthy financial habits for a lifetime.

Format

Each discussion guide is designed to take approximately 45 minutes to 1 hour to complete (not including time for fellowship and prayer). Each session includes...

Opening (1-2 minutes)

- **The Big Idea**: Summarizes the main takeaway for each week's study.
- **Key Verses:** Verses that inform that week's study. Many of these will be referenced in the discussion questions.
- **Opening Prayer:** This prayer is repeated in each study, inviting the Holy Spirit to lead you in this journey. To ensure you have time to complete the study, we recommend saving any personal prayer requests until the closing prayer.

Reflect and Share (3-5 minutes)

Starting in your second session, invite participants to share how they've seen the Holy Spirit at work in their financial thoughts, decisions and prayers since the last time you met.

Teaching Video (3-5 minutes)

These short videos (for chapters 1 to 6) reinforce the content covered throughout the chapter, sometimes using alternate illustrations

to share the same point. All of the teaching videos can be found at MoneySpirit.org.

Discussion (30-45 minutes)

Discussion questions help build an understanding of the content covered through the book and videos. They also invite participants to share what they are learning and to think about how they can apply these teachings to their own lives.

Prayer (3-5 minutes, or longer)

Allow participants to share personal prayer requests and praises. Read over the Prayer of Surrender that corresponds to the chapter being discussed, then pray over any personal requests and praises that have been shared.

Helpful Tips for Facilitators

You do not need to be an accomplished leader, teacher or expert who knows all the answers to facilitate this study! You simply need to be willing and available.

To make the most of your study, follow these best practices:

1. Pray, pray, pray! This study is all about surrendering to the work of the Holy Spirit. Listen for God's voice, and follow His lead.

2. Host your study in a private, comfortable location that is free from distractions and where everyone can feel safe sharing their personal experiences.

3. Find a day and time when you can consistently meet, preferably weekly or every other week. Do your best to stick to this schedule so that everyone can plan ahead. If you meet with a large group, you're bound to have conflicts—so decide if, when and how you'll decide to postpone or cancel. (For

example, "As long as two people are available to come, we'll meet.")

4. Build in extra time for fellowship before or after the study, but make sure you allow at least 45 minutes for the study itself. Start on time, every time, to honor the schedules of all participants.

5. Encourage everyone to bring their Bibles or to have a Bible app open on their phones. There will be several opportunities to read Scripture and discuss how it applies.

6. For chapters 1 through 6, try to have technology set up in advance so that you can view the teaching videos together as a group. If this is cumbersome or impossible in your situation, remind everyone to watch the videos prior to meeting. All the teaching videos can be found at MoneySpirit.org.

7. Model transparency! People have often treated money as a touchy topic—but it doesn't need to be. If you share openly, others will feel free to do the same.

8. Build trust by honoring each other's privacy. What's shared in confidence should be held in confidence.

9. Listen more than you talk. Become comfortable with awkward silence. Create space for everyone to share, including those who are more introverted by nature.

10. Show grace and adapt! Your study will not look like any study that's ever been done—or any that will ever happen again. If something's not working, change it. If something's working, run with it. Let go of any preconceived notions and be open to whatever God wants to do in and through you!

Introduction:
The Battle Within

The Big Idea

God wants to bring you freedom amidst whatever hopeless situation you face.

Key Verses

Although I want to do good, evil is right there with me. For in my inner being, I delight in God's law, but I see another law at work in me, waging war against the law of my mind and making me a prisoner of the law of sin within me. What a wretched man I am! Who will rescue me from this body that is subject to death? Thanks be to God, who delivers me through Jesus Christ our Lord!

Romans 7:21b-25

"No one can serve two masters. Either he will hate the one and love the other, or he will be devoted to the one and despise the other. You cannot serve both God and money."
Matthew 6:24

Opening Prayer

Lord, open our eyes and soften our hearts to the truth you want to reveal to us today. In Jesus's name, amen.

Discussion

1. Read Romans 7:21-25 together as a group. In what ways do you relate to Paul's struggle?
2. What parallels do you see between the preschooler's power struggle and our reluctance to follow God's direction?
3. In this introduction, the author describes how the word "money" is often treated as profanity in the church. Do you agree? Why or why not?
4. Did any of the statistics listed about our collective financial troubles surprise you? Why or why not?
5. In what ways have you seen money create bondage, both inside and outside the church walls?

6. Read Matthew 6:24. Why do you think Jesus talked about money so much, including in this verse?

7. How are you feeling about exploring financial surrender with this group in the weeks ahead? Excited? Fearful? Skeptical? Guarded?

8. Reread this question:

   "What if we all broke the stigma, stopped hiding, and started asking for God's will to be done in the areas where we need Him the most?"

   How might it change your life, your family, or your church if there were more transparency about our finances and a willingness to surrender them to the work of the Holy Spirit?

9. Were there any other parts of this introduction that stood out to you in any way?

Prayer

Have someone read the Prayer of Surrender found at the end of the introduction, and then close this session by praying for any additional needs of the group.

Chapter 1:
Good Fruit vs. Bad Fruit

The Big Idea

Money is spiritual—and so our money problems require spiritual solutions.

Key Verses

Walk by the Spirit, and you will not gratify the desires of the flesh.

Galatians 5:16

But the fruit of the Spirit is love, joy, peace, forbearance, kindness, goodness, faithfulness, gentleness and self-control. Against such things there is no law.

Galatians 5:22-23

Opening Prayer

Lord, open our eyes and soften our hearts to the truth you want to reveal to us today. In Jesus's name, amen.

Reflect and Share

Since we last met, in what ways have you seen the Holy Spirit at work in your thoughts, decisions or behaviors around money?

Teaching Video

Watch the video titled, "Good Fruit vs. Bad Fruit" found at MoneySpirit.org and then discuss these questions with your partner or group.

Discussion

1. This chapter and video offered several examples of "financial rot:" debt, greed, secrets, fears, and

disappointments. Where do you see evidence of these "bad fruit" in our world?

2. Can you think of a time when a poor financial decision left you or someone you know with a spoiled or bitter aftertaste?

3. What does the author mean by saying money decisions are spiritual decisions? Do you agree? In what ways does Josh's story resonate with your own journey as a believer?

4. Do you think Josh's pastor was out of line to talk about finances? Why or why not?

5. What were some of the biggest changes Josh experienced through surrender?

6. Reread Galatians 5:22-23. Which of these fruits would you like to see more evident in your finances?

7. What would the first (or next) step look like for you to surrender your finances to Jesus?

8. Were there any other parts of this chapter that stood out to you in any way?

Prayer

Have someone read the Prayer of Surrender found on page 11, and then close this session by praying for any additional needs of the group.

Chapter 2:
Love

The Big Idea

As God's love flows down into every part of our lives, we'll experience a confidence and security we've never known.

Key Verses

Now this is what the Lord Almighty says: "Give careful thought to your ways. You have planted much, but harvested little. You eat, but never have enough. You drink, but never have your fill. You put on clothes, but are not warm. You earn wages, only to put them in a purse with holes in it."

Haggai 1:5-6

I pray that out of his glorious riches he may strengthen you with power through his Spirit in your inner being, so that Christ may dwell in your hearts through faith. And I pray that you, being rooted and established in love, may have power, together with all the Lord's holy people, to grasp how wide and long and high and deep is the love of Christ, and to know this love that surpasses knowledge—that you may be filled to the measure of all the fullness of God.

Ephesians 3:16-19

Whoever loves money never has enough; whoever loves wealth is never satisfied with their income. This too is meaningless.

Ecclesiastes 5:10

Opening Prayer

Lord, open our eyes and soften our hearts to the truth you want to reveal to us today. In Jesus's name, amen.

Reflect and Share

Since we last met, in what ways have you seen the Holy Spirit at work in your thoughts, decisions or behaviors around money?

Teaching Video

Watch the video titled, "Love" found at MoneySpirit.org and then discuss these questions with your partner or group.

Discussion

1. Read Haggai 1:5-6 and Ecclesiastes 5:10. What modern-day parallels do you see in the world around you?

2. Can you think of a time when financial abundance or a purchase left you feeling empty?

3. Read the symptoms of a lack of affection listed on page 20. How might these symptoms manifest themselves in someone's financial decisions or behaviors?

4. How did you feel reading the love letter written on page 29? Was it difficult for you to imagine God speaking these verses directly to you? Why or why not?

5. Read Paul's prayer in Ephesians 3:16-19. In what ways would our financial decisions change if we

truly understood the love of Christ and found our worth in Him alone?

6. In what ways did Lance and Amy experience God's love in the middle of their struggle?

7. Has God ever asked you to do or surrender something that didn't make sense at the time? What did you learn in the process?

8. How might recognizing God's love and provision in our own lives change how we use our resources to bless others?

9. Were there any other parts of this chapter that stood out to you in any way?

Prayer

Have someone read the Prayer of Surrender found on page 30, and then close this session by praying for any additional needs of the group.

Chapter 3:
Joy and Peace

The Big Idea

Regardless of how much or how little we have, we can have peace and joy in our finances.

Key Verses

"Come to me, all you who are weary and burdened, and I will give you rest. Take my yoke upon you and learn from me, for I am gentle and humble in heart, and you will find rest for your souls. For my yoke is easy and my burden is light."

Matthew 11:28-30

Do not be anxious about anything, but in every situation, by prayer and petition, with thanksgiving, present your requests to God. And the peace of God, which transcends all understanding, will guard your hearts and your minds in Christ Jesus.

Philippians 4:6-7

Finally, brothers and sisters, whatever is true, whatever is noble, whatever is right, whatever is pure, whatever is lovely, whatever is admirable—if anything is excellent or praiseworthy—think about such things.

Philippians 4:8

Opening Prayer

Lord, open our eyes and soften our hearts to the truth you want to reveal to us today. In Jesus's name, amen.

Reflect and Share

Since we last met, in what ways have you seen the Holy Spirit at work in your thoughts, decisions or behaviors around money?

Teaching Video

Watch the video titled, "Joy and Peace" found at MoneySpirit.org and then discuss these questions with your partner or group.

Discussion

1. In the video, you were challenged to think of one word that comes to mind when you think about your current financial situation. What was your word?

2. Have you ever experienced a financial setback over which you felt you had no control?

3. In what ways has financial anxiety or discouragement affected your relationships?

4. Read Matthew 11:28-30 and Philippians 4:6-7. Share about a time when you were overwhelmed, worried or discouraged and then you brought the circumstances to God in prayer. What was that like? How did you feel? What did you learn? What did it change?

5. In this chapter, it said that daily gratitude lists are frequently used as part of the treatment plans for

patients with anxiety, depression and addictions. Why do you think that is?

6. Read Philippians 4:8. What are some practical ways you could build a habit of gratitude and redirect your thoughts to what God has in store for you?

7. Susan said, "God's always got something better for us than what we can see in those moments." Do you agree? Why or why not?

8. When it comes to financial literacy and foundational habits (budgeting, saving, debt repayment, etc.), what are some resources or other support that you or someone you know has found helpful in the past?

9. In what ways could God use your experiences of His peace and joy to be a blessing to others?

10. Were there any other parts of this chapter that stood out to you in any way?

Prayer

Have someone read the Prayer of Surrender found on page 51, and then close this session by praying for any additional needs of the group.

Chapter 4:
Patience and Self-Control

The Big Idea

There is sweet satisfaction in trusting God to provide what we need, at the proper time.

Key Verses

For the flesh desires what is contrary to the Spirit, and the Spirit what is contrary to the flesh. They are in conflict with each other, so that you are not to do whatever you want.

Galatians 5:17

I know what it is to be in need, and I know what it is to have plenty. I have learned the secret of being content in any and every situation, whether well fed or hungry, whether living in plenty or in want. I can do all this through him who gives me strength.

Philippians 4:12-13

Opening Prayer

Lord, open our eyes and soften our hearts to the truth you want to reveal to us today. In Jesus's name, amen.

Reflect and Share

Since we last met, in what ways have you seen the Holy Spirit at work in your thoughts, decisions or behaviors around money?

Teaching Video

Watch the video titled, "Patience and Self-Control" found at MoneySpirit.org and then discuss these questions with your partner or group.

Discussion

1. Have you ever bought something you felt you "needed" in the moment, but then you later regretted that purchase? What made it so difficult

to distinguish between "need" and "want" at the time?

2. In what kinds of situations are you most likely to overspend?

3. Read Galatians 5:17. How does this stand in contrast to the common sentiment, "Follow your heart"?

4. What does the Bible teach us about contentment? How does this differ from what the world promotes?

5. How do patience and self-control change the way we manage money?

6. Willie and Tina faced new financial constraints due to situations outside of their control. Have you ever had to tighten your budget? What were some of the things you learned in the process?

7. Explain what Willie meant by this statement: "We became investors of our money, instead of just spenders." Why did that make a difference for them?

8. Willie and Tina prioritized tithes and offerings in building their budget, setting that aside from the beginning. Why do you think that was?

9. In what ways can establishing boundaries offer us greater freedom, especially in our finances? What kind of boundaries might help you?

10. Read Philippians 4:10-13. This passage ends with a well-known Bible verse that is frequently quoted on its own. How does reading it in this context influence your understanding of Philippians 4:13?

11. Were there any other parts of this chapter that stood out to you in any way?

Prayer

Have someone read the Prayer of Surrender found on page 67, and then close this session by praying for any additional needs of the group.

Chapter 5:
Kindness and Gentleness

The Big Idea

In God's kingdom, money is a tool we can use to bless the lives of others.

Key Verses

"But who am I, and who are my people, that we should be able to give as generously as this? Everything comes from you, and we have given you only what comes from your hand."

1 Chronicles 29:14

You, my brothers and sisters, were called to be free. But do not use your freedom to indulge the flesh; rather, serve one another humbly in love.

Galatians 5:13

Therefore, as God's chosen people, holy and dearly loved, clothe yourselves with compassion, kindness, humility, gentleness and patience.
Colossians 3:12

Opening Prayer

Lord, open our eyes and soften our hearts to the truth you want to reveal to us today. In Jesus's name, amen.

Reflect and Share

Since we last met, in what ways have you seen the Holy Spirit at work in your thoughts, decisions or behaviors around money?

Teaching Video

Watch the video titled, "Kindness and Gentleness" found at MoneySpirit.org and then discuss these questions with your partner or group.

Discussion

1. How have you seen money used as a means to gain power, control or influence?

2. Read Psalm 24:1 and 1 Chronicles 29:10-16. How do these passages run in contrast to stories of the "self-made man" or the person who "pulled themselves up by their bootstraps"?

3. What assumptions might outsiders make about those who live in the Roseland neighborhood? How does knowing their history change that perception?

4. In what ways is Roseland Christian Ministries' invitation to "come as you are" a reflection of God's kindness and gentleness?

5. Has God ever spoken or ministered to you through someone else's kindness? What were the circumstances? How did you feel? What impact did it have on you?

6. Where do you tend to struggle more: giving freely to others without condition OR accepting the kindness of others toward you? Why?

7. How did seeing Joe through God's eyes change Sue's perspective?

8. Are there people you would treat differently if you looked at them the way God sees them?

9. What are some practical ways you can live out God's kindness and gentleness through your finances?

10. Were there any other parts of this chapter that stood out to you in any way?

Prayer

Have someone read the Prayer of Surrender found on page 84, and then close this session by praying for any additional needs of the group.

Chapter 6:
Goodness & Faithfulness

The Big Idea

As managers of God's resources, obedience to Jesus is everything.

Key Verses

"By their fruit you will recognize them. Do people pick grapes from thorn bushes, or figs from thistles? Likewise, every good tree bears good fruit, but a bad tree bears bad fruit."

Matthew 7:16-17

Whoever sows to please their flesh, from the flesh will reap destruction; whoever sows to please the Spirit, from the Spirit will reap eternal life. Let us not become weary in doing good, for at the proper time we will reap a harvest if we do not give up.

Galatians 6:8-9

Opening Prayer

Lord, open our eyes and soften our hearts to the truth you want to reveal to us today. In Jesus's name, amen.

Reflect and Share

Since we last met, in what ways have you seen the Holy Spirit at work in your thoughts, decisions or behaviors around money?

Teaching Video

Watch the video titled, "Goodness and Faithfulness" found at MoneySpirit.org and then discuss these questions with your partner or group.

Discussion

1. Read Matthew 7:16-17. What are some of the "thorns" and "thistles" you might expect to see in

the finances of someone who's lost sight of what's right and wrong?

2. Have you ever felt the pressure to cut corners or withhold information to get ahead financially?

3. Have you ever been tempted to justify poor or shady financial decisions according to what others are doing?

4. What does it change when we view God's goodness and faithfulness as the plumb line?

5. If we truly believe God is the owner of everything, and we are His stewards, how should this affect the ways we view and handle our money?

6. What were the ground rules Philip and Rachel set for themselves? How might you apply one or more of these rules to your own life?

7. Read Galatians 6:8-9. What are some practical ways you can remind yourself to "not become weary" in following the promptings of the Holy Spirit to do good?

8. What are some ways we can make it right when we fall short of reflecting God's goodness and faithfulness?

9. Were there any other parts of this chapter that stood out to you in any way?

Prayer

Have someone read the Prayer of Surrender found on page 98 and then close this session by praying for any additional needs of the group.

Chapter 7:
What's Your Story?

The Big Idea

There is no greater evidence of God at work than a transformed life.

Key Verses

"You are the light of the world. A town built on a hill cannot be hidden. Neither do people light a lamp and put it under a bowl. Instead they put it on its stand, and it gives light to everyone in the house. In the same way, let your light shine before others, that they may see your good deeds and glorify your Father in heaven."

Matthew 5:14

"If you love me, keep my commands. And I will ask the Father, and he will give you another advocate to help you and be with you forever— the Spirit of truth. The world cannot

accept him, because it neither sees him nor knows him. But you know him, for he lives with you and will be in you. I will not leave you as orphans; I will come to you."

John 14:15-18

"I have much more to say to you, more than you can now bear. But when he, the Spirit of truth, comes, he will guide you into all the truth. He will not speak on his own; he will speak only what he hears, and he will tell you what is yet to come."

John 16:12-13

Opening Prayer

Lord, open our eyes and soften our hearts to the truth you want to reveal to us today. In Jesus's name, amen.

Reflect and Share

Since we last met, in what ways have you seen the Holy Spirit at work in your thoughts, decisions or behaviors around money?

Discussion

1. Jesus often told stories and parables when teaching His disciples. Why do you think He did this?

2. What are some of the stories throughout this book that have resonated with your personal experiences or that have been particularly encouraging for your financial journey?

3. The author lists several excuses people make about why they can't share their stories with others. Can you relate to any of these?

4. How might the "feel, felt, found" method help you in sharing your spiritual journey with others?

5. Who are some of the people in your life—friends, children, coworkers, family, etc.—who might benefit from seeing and hearing how God has been at work through your finances?

6. Were there any other parts of this chapter that stood out to you in any way?

7. What are your biggest takeaways from this journey through "Money and Spirit"?

8. Practice sharing your story! Here are some prompts to guide you.

   - When it comes to your finances, where have you struggled?
   - What evidence of rotten fruit have you seen in your life?

- In what ways have you experienced God at work in you throughout this study?
- What spiritual fruit do you see growing in the ways you view and manage God's money?
- What do you think the Holy Spirit is still trying to teach you?

Prayer

Have someone read the Prayer of Surrender found on page 122, and then close this session by praying for any additional needs of the group.

We'd Love to Hear Your Story!

What has the Holy Spirit revealed to you through this study? How are you seeing His fruit in your finances? We'd love to hear from you!

Visit MoneySpirit.org to share your story today.

Acknowledgments

I t has been my joy and honor to write this book on behalf of Barnabas Foundation. Through this ministry, I have been equipped to grow in so many ways, including as a writer, leader, steward, and child of God.

Additionally, this book is the byproduct of a deep well of wisdom and support from my wonderful community! In particular, I would like to extend a special thank you to the following people and organizations:

- The Lilly Foundation, which provided critical funding through a grant to the Financial Shalom Project, making this book and the accompanying study guide and videos possible.
- John Bolt and the leadership of the Christian Reformed Church of North America for entrusting us to be part of the Financial Shalom Project and for your ongoing partnership in Kingdom-building ministry.

- The Morgan James team for taking a chance on a new author and for all your support along the way to make this dream come true.
- The brilliant and talented Megan Pacheco and Kasia Tunnell, whose surrender to the voice of the Holy Spirit sparked the original idea for this project. The powerful writing and creative work you did with Wes Shelnutt and John Greco for the videos also created a solid foundation on which this book was built. Thank you, thank you, thank you.
- Jordan Hansen for elevating the visual impact of the study group videos. Your creative talent consistently amazes me!
- Josh, Laura, Lance, Amy, Philip, Rachel, Susan, Willie, Tina, Joe, Sue, Kadie and Roseland Christian Ministries for allowing us to tell your stories.
- LaMorris and Megan Crawford, a.k.a. the "prophets at Applebee's." Thank you for consistently listening to God's voice and acting on His behalf. So many lives have been changed as a result—including mine. Thank you!
- My pastors Ken Bushey, Ken and Teresa Garner, Susan Armstrong and Jack McCormick whose sermons and wisdom over the years have

undoubtedly shaped my understanding of the Holy Spirit and infiltrated the pages of the book.

- My dear church family at Manteno Church of the Nazarene for teaching, loving and supporting my family in a thousand different ways. Thank you for embodying our shared mission to love God, journey together, serve others, and share Jesus.

- Lisa Thomson, for your outstanding editing skills and insightful feedback that helped refine and improve my original manuscript in so many ways.

- Lucas Pospychala, for your thorough, thoughtful and repeated reviews of this manuscript and for your humble, kindhearted, quality work on which I so frequently depend.

- My friend and former coworker, Rev. Phillip Leo. It would be impossible to overstate how your thoughtful questions, ideas, corrections, written contributions, affirmations and prayers shaped the trajectory of this book. Thank you for your wisdom and grace, on the good days and the hard. I'm sorry I couldn't work an analogy about the 7-Day War into these pages.

- Barnabas Foundation's marketing team and all my incredible co-workers throughout the organization for your encouragement, prayers and assistance throughout the 84 years this project seemed to take.

- James Bakke, executive director of Barnabas Foundation, for believing in this project and for providing me with the resources and bandwidth to accomplish it. Thanks also for your outstanding leadership and insightful feedback that always makes my work better (even when, and especially when, I'm being defensive).

- My parents, Rev. Mike and Becky Quimby, for treating everything I've ever written as works of art and for modeling what it looks like to live in complete surrender to the Holy Spirit. I am so blessed to have you as my champions and my heroes!

- My amazing kids, Emma and Jackson, who have always kept me humble and laughing. Thanks for being so awesome and for providing me with a lifetime of anecdotes through the daily absurdity of being your mother. You're both my favorites!

- My handsome husband, Robert, whose sage and timely advice to "stop worrying so much about the details and just write from your heart" got me unstuck. Thanks for your encouragement and for keeping the kids fed, busy and at their various activities when I was out-of-pocket. More importantly, thank you for your constant love and faithfulness as my God-given partner on the journey of surrender. There's no one I'd rather travel this road with than you.

Above all, my deepest gratitude and devotion belong to God the Father, God the Son, and God the Holy Spirit.

Every single one of my spiritual fruits were squeezed throughout this project, and I'm grateful for the lessons you have taught me along the way (including the ones about patience and self-control). You've given me life and purpose. You've loved me when I was unlovable. You gave me words when there were none.

God, this project has always been, and will always be, for you. Do with it what you'd like.

About Barnabas Foundation

Since 1976, Barnabas Foundation has helped thousands of generous Christians transfer their wealth in ways that honor God, provide for their families and support the ministries close to their hearts.

Learn More
BarnabasFoundation.org
info@BarnabasFoundation.org
888.448.3040

About the Author

Heather M. Day is writer, editor and communication specialist with more than 20 years of experience in the fields of marketing, public relations and fundraising.

Passionate about ministry, Heather has spent the bulk of her career in the nonprofit arena, including in her current role as Director of Marketing for Barnabas Foundation. In this role, she provides marketing strategy and resources to more than 200 nonprofit Christian ministries.

Previously, Heather served as Director of Marketing Communications for Olivet Nazarene University, Director of Communications for Lead Like Jesus, and Creative Services Coordinator for Bible League International. She holds a bachelor's degree in Communications and an Executive MBA from Olivet Nazarene University.

Heather and her husband, Robert, reside in Bourbonnais, IL with their two children, Emma and Jackson. She is an active member, board member and volunteer leader at Manteno Church of the Nazarene.

Learn more at HeatherDay.net.

A free ebook edition
is available with the
purchase of this book.

To claim your free ebook edition:

1. Visit MorganJamesBOGO.com
2. Sign your name CLEARLY in the space
3. Complete the form and submit a photo of the entire copyright page
4. You or your friend can download the ebook to your preferred device

Print & Digital Together Forever.

Snap a photo

Free ebook

Read anywhere

Printed in the USA
CPSIA information can be obtained
at www.ICGtesting.com
JSHW081107011024
70760JS00005B/9